DO THIS. NOT THAT.

CAREER

What to DO (and NOT DO) in 75+ Difficult Workplace Situations

Jenny Foss

ADAMS MEDIA

NEW YORK LONDON TORONTO SYDNEY NEW DELHI

Adams Media
An Imprint of Simon & Schuster, Inc.
100 Technology Center Drive
Stoughton, Massachusetts 02072

First Adams Media hardcover edition January 2023

ADAMS MEDIA and colophon are trademarks of Simon & Schuster.

For information about special discounts for bulk purchases, please contact Simon & Schuster Special Sales at 1-866-506-1949 or business@simonandschuster.com.

The Simon & Schuster Speakers Bureau can bring authors to your live event. For more information or to book an event contact the Simon & Schuster Speakers Bureau at 1-866-248-3049 or visit our website at www.simonspeakers.com.

Interior design by Colleen Cunningham

Manufactured in China

10 9 8 7 6 5 4 3 2 1

Library of Congress Cataloging-in-Publication Data has been applied for.

ISBN 978-1-5072-1966-9
ISBN 978-1-5072-1967-6 (ebook)

CONTENTS

5 Handling Other Workplace Dilemmas 150

INTRODUCTION

If you've been doing:

LESS OF THIS:
finding the perfect job...

...AND MORE OF THAT:
receiving one too many "Unfortunately, the position has already been filled" messages...

Or you wish you were:

DOING THIS:
building positive relationships with your boss and coworkers...

...INSTEAD OF THAT:
dealing with micro-managers and colleagues who undermine you...

You're in the right place.

For a lot of people, finding a job and managing your career can feel confusing—and about as much fun as food poisoning. The good news is that you're *not* stuck in a job you hate—and it *is* possible to get along with your boss and coworkers. You just need a little guidance in doing *this*— and not *that*—to become better at handling your career!

Do This, Not That: Career is a straightforward and easy-to-use guide that will help you navigate the modern workplace, gain the confidence to go after what you want, and build the career you dream about. How exactly? Not by luck or chance, but instead by focusing on preparing yourself for the job hunt, conducting yourself professionally, and advancing your career with raises and promotions: the keys for a successful career.

And because careers aren't one size fits all, this book isn't *all* about telling you what to do; rather, it asks you questions and helps you explore your personal experiences so you can make the right choices for *you*. Organized into chapters based on themes like finding a new job, dealing with your boss, and handling common workplace dilemmas, you'll identify what to do (and not do) in eighty-one situations, including when:

- You apply for a new job but aren't a 100 percent fit
- You want to ask for a promotion or raise
- You want to be friends with your coworkers outside of the workplace
- You want to reassure employees during a difficult time
- You discover your job is nothing like described in the interview
- You need to figure out if it's time to find a new job
- And much more

You're going to understand the most effective ways to find and keep a job you love, and finally feel ready to build the career you deserve! So let's do *this*, not *that*.

HOW TO USE THIS BOOK

Do This, Not That: Career is your guide to dealing with various difficult career situations. It will help you to confidently navigate the ups and downs of the modern workplace. You can dip into this book when you're not sure of what to do in a specific situation; just flip through to the scenario that applies to you. Or, if you want to get your PhD in career management, you can read the book cover to cover.

Each career scenario is divided into sections—*as seen on the right*—for a comprehensive, actionable guide to handling that situation.

Each scenario is also organized under a main theme of careers, so you can easily find guidance on whatever obstacle you are facing. Whether you are looking to find a new job, establish a great relationship with your boss, connect with your coworkers, take your career to the next level with a promotion, handle tricky workplace situations, or deal with something in between, there is advice for you.

Every decision you make about your career is your own; this book will ask you the right questions to help you arrive at the best solution for you. It will guide you in making decisions about the right time to move on to a new job, how to deal with a nosy colleague, and even how to become the boss yourself.

First, you'll find tips for how to deal with the problem at hand.

 Next, you'll explore big no-nos to avoid if you want your career to unfold smoothly.

✓ **HERE'S HOW** Then, you'll find clear action steps to tackle the situation, from what to say if, for example, you don't agree with a decision your boss has made, to how to have a positive mindset during a difficult time, like if you get laid off.

Think This:

This section gives you a mindset for dealing with your career problem in a way that's calm and confident. The advice here will help you feel less anxious, overwhelmed, or confused.

Say This:

You can use one of these example phrases as a model when communicating with your boss, coworkers, or in some cases yourself. Choose the phrase that best fits your situation: Remember that the advice that's right for you will be based on your individual circumstances. These catchphrases are there to inspire you as you encounter various career challenges, but feel free to put them into your own words. Successful workplace communication should never feel like you're reading from a script.

WHAT NEXT? ⟶

Once you start thinking about your career in a way that is calm and confident, rather than anxious and overwhelmed, you'll be ready to embrace next steps for moving forward and getting what you want.

Chapter 1

FINDING AND STARTING A NEW JOB

We all want career fulfillment, jobs that are challenging and rewarding, that pay well, and that allow us to grow professionally while having plenty of time and energy left in the tank for our personal lives. We want to work with people we like and admire, in environments that are warm, supportive, and, yes, also fun.

Is that too much to ask for? No! But the truth is, finding and landing these jobs—and making sure you're successful right from the start—can be a daunting undertaking. There's a lot to navigate—from determining how (or if) you should apply, to mastering the various types of interviews, to negotiating your job offer, to making a great first impression and getting to know your boss and coworkers. That's where this chapter comes in.

In this chapter, you'll find dozens of tips that'll take you from the moment you find a job advertisement that piques your interest to your first days and weeks in your brand-new role. You'll find answers to some of the most common questions people have when shifting jobs, including those related to cover letters, compensation, and company culture. You'll also learn how to network effectively with people working at a company of interest, sashay your way through interview blunders, score a competitive offer, and ensure you're equipped to knock it out of the park as you settle in.

Job searching is a lot of work, but it's also an exciting time full of opportunities to showcase your many skills, interests, and goals. Let's do this.

You Want to Apply for a New Job but Aren't a 100 Percent Fit

You find a job advertisement that looks incredible, and you *know* you'd be amazing in the role. But you're not a perfect match for their requirements. Maybe they're looking for five years of experience, and you have precisely three. Perhaps they need an Excel power user, and that's not you. Should you still apply?

 Try these ideas to address this issue:

1 **If you meet 70 percent or more of the requirements, give it a shot.**
That's covering enough of the necessary skills to make it worth applying.

2 **Shift your resume messaging to better clarify your fit.**
For example, if you're applying for a project management job but have never held that title, point out instances in your career when you've managed projects.

3 **Mirror the keywords you see in the job description.**
If a job calls for digital marketing and customer service skills, and you've got both, but your resume says "social media marketing" and "client relations," switch to their wording. Keywords are crucial in online applications.

4 **Find an "in" at the company.**
Talk to people! If you really want to work at a certain company, go on the offense and get to know people who may help pave the way.

5 **Create a memorable presentation or additional materials for the hiring manager.**
If this is your dream job, don't rely just on that generic online application everyone's using. Try creating a standout presentation that *shows* the reviewer what you'd bring to the table.

DON'T LOSE ALL SIGHT OF REALITY. There is a difference between a thoughtful gamble and a pipe dream. If your dream is to be a lawyer and you've never been to law school, no amount of creativity, schmoozing, or resume massaging is going to take you the distance. If you're missing "must-have" baseline credentials, hatch a plan to acquire them or think about related jobs that might be a great foot-in-the-door to an industry of interest.

HERE'S HOW Now that you're armed with a few "dos" and a giant "don't," consider these additional tips as you apply for that role.

Think This:

"I won't let fears hold me back." If you're like many people, you're a little bit afraid of rejection or of looking stupid applying for a job you're not fully qualified for. Don't let either of these fears hold you back if you feel strongly about an opportunity of interest. It's unlikely that any applicant is a perfect fit, so remind yourself that you have as much of a right to apply as any other candidate. Try to stay positive!

Say This:

"I suspect the _____ experience I'd bring from my current job (or education, or volunteer work) would be incredibly beneficial. Here's why…"

"While I've not yet formally held that title, I'm actually doing a lot of this work right now. Here are a few details from a recent project…"

"I saw that you're looking for strong Excel skills, so I've enrolled in an advanced Excel workshop to ensure I'm current in VLOOKUP and PivotTables."

WHAT NEXT? ⟶

If you put your best foot forward and land an interview, amazing! Now it's time to do your homework and prepare. If you get the dreaded "thanks, but no thanks" letter (ugh), dust yourself off, get back up again, and think about how you might fine-tune your approach the next time. You can also ask the hiring manager for feedback on how you might have been a stronger candidate. Remember, one rejection does not define you. When you take risks to stretch and grow, rejection may happen. Give yourself a high five for putting yourself out there and keep pressing forward.

You Don't Know How to Do an Informational Interview

Informational interviews are conversations you can have with people working in an industry—or at a company—of interest as you explore potential job opportunities. They can give you a leg up when you're looking for a job—forging an "in" at a company of interest is a great way to connect with potential colleagues or mentors and be referred for a job. But you're worried. You've never done one before, and you don't want to look overly needy, pesky, or like a complete newbie. So, how do you make sure your informational interview is a smashing success?

 Try these ideas to address this issue:

1 **Keep the initial request short, sweet, and no more than a few sentences long.**
Explain who you are (and if you were referred by someone), what your career goal is, and why you're reaching out. And, when you ask for their time, request no more than 15–20 minutes for the session.

2 **Remember that *you* are the interviewer, not the interviewee.**
Come to the call or meeting prepared with at least four or five questions about the person, their team, their work, and/or the company.

3 **Allow the conversation to flow.**
It'll be more enjoyable for both of you if it's a natural, easygoing chat where you follow up and show you understand things, versus a rapid-fire ping-pong match of question/answer/question/answer. At the end of the conversation, ask this final question: "Based on our discussion, can you think of anyone else I should introduce myself to?" (Let's keep this going!)

4 **Send a thank-you email right after the meeting.**
Also, assuming you benefit from any advice that was shared, be sure to follow up with the good news. People love feeling valuable and appreciated.

DON'T TRY TO TURN THIS INTO A JOB INTERVIEW, no matter how badly you want to work for this company. Repeat after me: This is not a job interview. It would be called that if it were. The informational interview is designed to help you gather information about a company, person, or industry of interest and, with luck, build relationships that may benefit you as you progress through your job search. While you should have your resume at the ready just in case, don't even think about foisting it on your interviewee unless you're specifically asked for it.

✔ HERE'S HOW

Now that you know what to do and what to avoid, use these tips to make your next informational interview a success.

Think This:

"I'm not imposing; I'm asking to benefit from their expertise and experience." Even if you're a bundle of nerves (deep breaths!), remind yourself that your interviewee wouldn't have agreed to the conversation if they weren't genuinely happy to share their knowledge and help you. (You could also think about how *you* might be a resource for someone else down the line!)

Say This:

"I'm curious; how did you get into this field?"

"What are the best parts about your job? What are the most challenging?"

"What skills would you say are the most important for someone trying to break into this field?"

"If you were in my position, what actions would you take first to prepare yourself for the job/industry?"

WHAT NEXT?

Once you've collected your information, it's time to determine if this position/company is right for you to pursue if any jobs open up. If it is, great! Consider following up with your contact for quick advice on how to put your best foot forward. If it isn't, ask yourself what about the information you received doesn't align with your career goals, and how you should proceed. No matter what you decide, informational interviews will be incredibly valuable in helping you fine-tune your strategy and determine where you should focus your efforts.

You Need Help Writing a Powerful Cover Letter

Writing an effective cover letter is hard for most people, but it's a necessary part of many job searches. Even if writing is not your forte, you can still craft a letter that conveys your passion for the position and expands on the information given in your resume. The basic procedure for writing a powerful cover letter is actually pretty simple once you get the hang of it. So how can you craft pitches that can outshine the competition?

 Try these ideas to address this issue:

1 **Create a strong lead.**
Start with a sentence or two that tells the reader right away that you're applying for this job because you admire the company and their products or services and would absolutely love to work there. Be genuine and specific!

2 **Provide clear evidence that you're a fit.**
Make sure it's obvious that you've got the skills and experience they're looking for. You could write something like this: "What, specifically, would I bring to [company name] in this role?" And then, follow it up with a few key points that highlight your core strengths (study the job description for hints of what skills and keywords you should mention).

3 **Finish strong.**
Tie things up in a way that says, "I believe my experience with X and knowledge of Y will enable me to quickly contribute to the team. I'd love to meet to learn more!"

DON'T PUT TOO MUCH FOCUS ON YOUR CAREER GOALS IN YOUR COVER LETTER. While it's crucial to honor them as you pursue new opportunities, at the earliest stages of the interview process, your future employer cares much more about what *they* need than what your goals are. Be sure to position your cover letter more toward what you can bring to this job versus what you're looking for. Certainly, your new boss will care a great deal about your needs and goals as you settle into the role. But at the application stage, make it about them.

✓ HERE'S HOW

Now that you've got the focus down, here are a few additional things to consider before you start writing.

Think This:	Say This:
"This is a marketing tool—one that I'm going to use to prompt my future employer to make a 'purchase decision.'" In this case, the purchase decision you're aiming for is "Invite you to an interview." Also, remind yourself that putting in some effort to customize your letters will help ensure your pitches are original, impactful, and stand out against the competition.	"Here's who I am, why I admire this company, and why I'm applying for this job." "Based on my understanding of what you need, here's why I'm a great match." "Here's what makes me interesting, likeable, and memorable." (Don't be shy about giving them a glimpse at your first-rate personality!)

WHAT NEXT? ⟶

If you can, find a direct contact to whom you can send your cover letter and resume. This will maximize the odds that it'll be read. If you can't find an obvious contact, you can attach the cover letter to the online application, but you'll have the best shot at captivating readers with a powerful cover letter when reaching out directly. Take advantage of *every* opportunity to outshine the competition as you apply for jobs of interest—including the opportunity to dazzle them with an amazing cover letter.

You Have Technology Issues Mid-Interview

Video interviews. Love 'em or hate 'em, they're here to stay. And, while it goes without saying that you'll need to prepare for both the conversation *and* the technical details when prepping for a virtual interview, do you know what to do if you hit a technological snag smack-dab in the middle of the discussion? (Hint: Panic is not the correct answer.)

 Try these ideas to address this issue:

1. **Check your equipment and your connection ahead of time.**
   Not sure if your microphone and webcam are working? Test them in advance. Also, make sure you're somewhere with a stable Internet connection. (Pro tip: Do a speed test, such as the one at www.speedtest.net, shortly before the interview.)

2. **Ask for the interviewer's phone number as you get started, just in case.**
   Establishing that plan B will give you peace of mind while illustrating your attention to detail.

3. **See if the chat function still works.**
   If you lose audio or video mid-interview, quickly check if you can still access the platform's chat feature. If yes, send a quick alert to your interviewer.

4. **Try restarting your modem.**
   Alternatively, if you can, connect directly to the router (the issue may be your Wi-Fi) and rejoin the meeting.

DON'T ASSUME THE SITUATION IS UNSALVAGEABLE. No matter how awkward things get—or how badly you think you perform following a technical glitch—you might be able to turn it around. Remember, there's a human on the other end of that call. They've probably had a similar moment themselves. If the call ends completely, reach out and ask for a second chance. There's also no need to grovel or overapologize. Simply let them know how excited you are about the opportunity and request a "Take 2" given the situation.

HERE'S HOW Now that you're equipped to respond to technology issues, here are a few additional suggestions to help you stay in the right frame of mind should they crop up.

Think This:

"Recruiters want me to succeed; that's how their performance is measured—open positions filled." Chances are your interviewers aren't ominous villains. And hiring managers have a business need going unmet so they are motivated to find the right people to assume those responsibilities. So if a tech issue compromises the conversation, remind yourself that all parties want this to work out; it's in everyone's interest to figure out the best way forward.

Say This:

"It appears my Zoom audio is malfunctioning. May I mute myself and call you instead?"

"I really appreciate your patience. May I disconnect and rejoin the meeting from another device?"

"I suspect this won't be resolved quickly. Might we reschedule within the next day or two?" (Getting the "do-over" booked right away is the best way.)

WHAT NEXT? ⟶

If your glitch was resolved relatively easily, try adding a bit of humor that acknowledges your challenges ("I swear I wasn't dodging that question about my PowerPoint skills when my Wi-Fi went out!") to your thank-you note. If you suspect that things still could've gone better, reiterate key points ("I blipped out just as I was sharing details of our 42 percent revenue growth last year."). And then, assuming you want the job, make sure they know you'd love to join the team!

Your Interviewer Asks about Your Salary Requirements

One of the hardest interview questions to answer is also one of the most common ones: "What salary are you looking for?" It's a Catch-22: If you throw out a number that's too high, you price yourself out of the running. If it's too low, you may land yourself a job...at a much lower salary than the company was willing to pay. So, how should you manage the dreaded salary question?

 Try these ideas to address this issue:

1 **Offer a range versus a number.**
Prepare in advance by researching the market and knowing your own financial situation so you can decide on your ideal salary range given your region, function, and experience. This way, you can present both high and lower numbers that are acceptable to you and in line with market rates.

2 **Explain yourself.**
When you present the range, explain how you came to it and outline the value you'll provide in return.

3 **Ask the question.**
If you'd rather they go first, try saying, "I'd love to discuss the position in more detail and outline how I could contribute. Did you have a range that you can share?" (This strategy doesn't always work, but you're in a stronger position to negotiate if they share numbers first.)

DON'T THROW OUT A NUMBER LOWER THAN YOU'RE WILLING TO ACCEPT (for fear that they won't consider you otherwise), and then insist on a higher salary once you realize the employer really wants to hire you. As you might imagine, this is not going to be viewed favorably and could, in fact, jeopardize your offer altogether. Think about if a company did the reverse to you. You'd be upset over being lowballed, right? Of course—so don't play games with the numbers. Present a number or range that's honest and realistic, and then demonstrate to everyone you meet with that you're worth the investment!

HERE'S HOW

Now that you know what to say in the moment, here are a few additional strategies to use the next time an interviewer asks how much you want to make.

Think This:

"I'm worth it." Talking about money can definitely be awkward. But tell yourself that you're worth your expected salary—your education, experience, hard work, and skills all led up to this moment. Adopt a mindset that discussing your salary is just another piece of the employment puzzle—you can treat the topic as matter-of-factly as you would health insurance options or vacation days.

Say This:

"Based on my market research, experience, and career goals, my range is between $65,000 and $80,000. Does this align with your budget?"

"My primary goal is to find a role that allows me to apply my strengths while positively impacting the environment. Would you be okay if we talk about your needs and my background before discussing numbers?"

WHAT NEXT?

If they're amenable to your salary request, terrific. If they push back on either the range or your request to talk money later, decide whether the opportunity is worth further exploration. Having clarity around your goals, confidence in your worth, and knowledge of what the market will bear will help you make the career decisions that are best for you.

You Botched the Interview but Really Want the Job

You researched and practiced before the interview, yet, somehow, you bombed it. (Or so you think.) Maybe you rambled, or froze, or inexplicably sounded like a robot. The possibilities are nearly endless when it comes to interview slipups, but the way they make you feel is universally awful. And it's even worse when you *really* wanted that job. So, what should you do if you interview poorly for a job that really matters to you?

 Try these ideas to address this issue:

1 **Reflect before you react.**
Before attempting damage control, play back the conversation as objectively as you can. Did you *really* flub up, or are you being hard on yourself? Empathetic interviewers know candidates are nervous and will offer some grace. You may not need to do anything except cut yourself a bit of slack.

2 **Use your thank-you note strategically.**
This is the perfect platform for addressing any mistakes you made, like experience you failed to mention or skills you have but forgot to highlight. Don't rattle on, but do make the most of this valuable opportunity to correct any oversights.

3 **Ask for another shot.**
This strategy is best suited for times in which extenuating circumstances negatively impacted performance (e.g., a sick child had you up all night, you got shocking news right before the interview, etc.). You may get a no, but they could say yes.

DON'T GROVEL. Unless you said or did something decidedly offensive, or completely missed the interview (in which case, a timely apology is merited), don't go overboard apologizing. In fact, that may put extra emphasis on the thing you botched and make an interviewer rethink your candidacy. Conversely, don't assume it's a lost cause and bury your head in the sand if you know you could have done better. Make every effort to salvage the operation. You're worth it!

✓ HERE'S HOW

Here are a few additional things to think, say, and do when dealing with a botched interview.

Think This:

"I shouldn't be too hard on myself." We are all our own worst critics, and job interviews can send even the most confident people into a tailspin of self-doubt and distress. Everyone makes mistakes, and everyone can improve. Embrace that opportunity to do better next time and investigate mindfulness techniques that may help you stay calm and confident when the heat is on.

Say This:

"You asked about my project management skills earlier, and I forgot to share these details from a customer event I planned and managed recently."

"While I've not used Salesforce yet, I've enrolled in an online Salesforce training and should have solid baseline knowledge by next week."

"I wasn't at my best because my spouse was ill, and I've been juggling a lot. Would you consider a do-over?"

WHAT NEXT?

If the interviewer responds favorably to your damage control, fantastic. Consider yourself lucky and work hard to perform to your absolute best through any remaining interview rounds. If you've given it your best shot and they say no, say thank you, let them know that you'd love to be considered should another relevant job open up, take the lesson from this experience, and move on with your head held high. And remember, life's sweetest successes are sometimes the ones that come only *after* a bit of adversity.

You Need to Provide References

As you move through the job interview process, you may be asked to provide your potential employer with references. This is a good sign! It means you're being strongly considered for the job. Your interviewers are ready to collect more information to help them finalize their decision. But who should your references be and how do you ask them to help you?

 Try these ideas to address this issue:

1. **Make your list of willing participants well in advance.**
Later, once you know more about specific roles, you can share the references you feel will be most relevant given the job—and most likely to help you land the offer.

2. **Choose relevant (professional) references.**
Most interviewers will strongly prefer speaking with people from your current or most recent employer, especially your supervisor(s). However, if you're a covert job seeker (and don't want your boss to know what's up), you may need to reach back a bit further, or ask a trusted colleague if they're willing to take the call.

3. **Ask for permission.**
Even if you've used someone as a reference before, it's common courtesy to touch base before listing them again.

4. **Make it easy on your interviewers by double-checking that all contact information is current.**
Also, share details on who the references are and your relationship to them.

5. **Brief your references on the job opportunities you're looking at.**
Tell them what you'd love for them to share. Thank them and don't forget to offer to reciprocate in the future.

DON'T WAIT UNTIL THE LAST MINUTE TO DRUM UP, APPROACH, AND PREP YOUR REFERENCES. When you're asked to provide them, chances are you're a finalist candidate. You don't want to jeopardize your top-contender status by asking the hiring manager to wait while you collect a list, making it challenging for a potential employer to get hold of your people, or by choosing references that won't commit to supporting you.

HERE'S HOW If you're still feeling a bit nervous or uncertain as you prepare to start contacting potential references, use this guidance to maximize the odds they'll say yes.

Think This:

"Asking for—and providing—references is a common business practice." So don't feel shy or self-conscious asking someone. People will likely be glad to support you! Think about positive performance reviews or kind emails you've received in the past—all you're asking is for someone to share the same feelings to a third party. Also, keep in mind that some companies have a policy that precludes employees from serving as references for current or former colleagues, so don't take it personally if someone says no.

Say This:

"Here's what I've been up to professionally since we last spoke" (if it's been a while since you last worked together).

"Here's why I'm excited about the role."

"Here's what's happening at the company (or on the team), and how I believe my skills and experience will be beneficial."

"Can I count on you to share a favorable review?"

WHAT NEXT?

Once your references have been contacted, express your sincere thanks to them and ask how it went. If they mention anything that gave the interviewer pause, consider giving your next reference a heads-up. Assuming it's honest to do so, ask them to emphasize your strengths in that area. Return the favor if your reference needs a reference!

You Want to Negotiate an Offer

You did it! You made it all the way through the interview process and you're reviewing a job offer. And that feels pretty amazing, except for one little thing: It isn't quite what you had in mind; you think you should negotiate. While the thought of negotiating can seem daunting, most organizations anticipate that candidates will present a counteroffer. And you already know they want you, so how can you confidently ask for what you're worth?

 Try these ideas to address this issue:

1 **Prepare a pitch.**
If certain aspects of the offer don't align with your expectations, put together a data-backed proposal outlining what you want, why you're requesting it, and what specific value you'll provide in exchange.

2 **Practice before presenting.**
While you definitely don't want to stall, if time permits, grab a friend and practice negotiating the offer before responding to your potential employer. (Know any recruiters or HR people? They'd be great options!)

3 **Share your enthusiasm.**
There's no need to become stern, detached, or adversarial when negotiating. Rather, as you roll out your counteroffer, make sure they know that you're excited to join the team and eager to make things official.

4 **Be ready for every possible response, including this one: "Sorry, this is our final offer."**
Hopefully, your negotiating will be fruitful, but know in advance what you'll do if they won't budge.

DON'T CHICKEN OUT AND BE AFRAID TO NEGOTIATE. The most important thing to remember if you feel strongly that you're worth more than you've been offered is this: You don't want to settle on an initial offer, then wish you hadn't. Respect yourself enough to ask for what you want and what you deserve. The worst they can say is no, so there's no harm in asking!

HERE'S HOW
Now that you've got the framework for negotiating the job offer, here are additional pointers that'll help you make this a productive discussion.

Think This:

"I'm holding a lot of the cards right now." Even if you're new to negotiating, you can bring some confidence to the table. After all, you've already won over your interviewers. (Trust me, they don't want to go through the time-consuming interview process all over again.) They anticipate your skills and experience will be valuable, and they see you as a great fit for the team. So get yourself ready, make a strong case, and then start planning for your first day on the job!

Say This:

"This is exciting! We're close. I'll be prepared to sign off and can start immediately if you can commit to a salary of $75,000."

"I understand you're at the top of your range. Could we get creative with total compensation to bring the offer in line with my experience and the range I'm looking for—perhaps a signing bonus or more stock options?"

"I'm eager to join the team. However, I've just received an offer of $85,000. Would you consider matching this?"

WHAT NEXT? ⟶

If your negotiations are successful, congratulations! Be sure to get everything in writing before resigning from your current role. If, despite your best efforts, the job offer still isn't coming together to your expectations, weigh the pros and cons of accepting the offer as is. Is there plenty of room for growth? Do you *really* love the company and team? If so, it may be worth a shot. If not, respectfully decline, thank everyone for their consideration, and move on confidently.

You Aren't Sure What to Wear on Your First Day

You've landed a new job and want to make sure you impress everyone right from the start. But as you ponder wardrobe options for day one, you're feeling rather stumped. Picking that winning outfit can feel especially confounding if your new role is virtual and the meet-and-greets will be via webcam. How can you choose clothes that will show off your personality and professionalism?

 Try these ideas to address this issue:

1 Ask your point person for suggestions.
You likely worked closely with a recruiter or had a main contact through the interview process. Ask them for the scoop on company dress code, or specific suggestions on what to wear.

2 Study what your future teammates wear.
If you can, think back on what your interviewers were wearing. Or check out their LinkedIn profiles to see what your soon-to-be peers consider professional attire.

3 Opt for low-key.
Of course, you should dress in a way that feels authentic to you, but for the first day, you might not want to choose your most unusual or surprising wardrobe pieces.

4 Wear something comfortable *and* easy to dress up or down.
This way, you can make an instant shift if you've gauged incorrectly. (Think: a blazer over a more casual shirt.)

DON'T USE "BUT, I'M BROKE" AS YOUR EXCUSE TO WEAR SOMETHING STAINED OR ILL-FITTING. Shop your closet, hit the local consignment store, or borrow from a friend. (And then make sure everything is clean, pressed, and/or polished.) There are so many places to find inexpensive clothing nowadays that you can no doubt put together a winning outfit on a budget. Also, don't stress too much about this decision. If you're comfortable and dressed in a way that is a match for your industry/company, you'll be fine.

HERE'S HOW

Beyond the basics, these tips and talking points will help you as you narrow down what to wear for your first day on the job.

Think This:

"What am I most comfortable in? What complements my personality? What helps me feel confident?" Day one will surely be exciting, and maybe a little stressful. Think about how your clothes can ease your stress and help you put your best foot forward. You don't want your outfit to be something you even have to really think about—you should be focused on learning the ropes and getting to know your colleagues.

Say This:

Ask yourself: "What do I feel really great in?"

Ask your recruiter (or new boss): "Do you have a dress code or recommendations on attire?"

Ask a clothing (or consignment) store associate: "How does this color/cut/style look on me?"

Ask your same-sized relative: "Can I borrow that blazer next Monday?"

Ask your stylish friend: "Will you help me put together a few options?"

WHAT NEXT?

If you land on that magical first-day outfit combination—it's comfortable and you feel great in it—you'll feel instantly at ease and be able to focus on the truly important things, like finding the bathroom and setting up your laptop. If you realize that you've missed the mark just a bit, try not to sweat it. Most people probably won't even notice, and you'll have plenty of time to fine-tune your look. Throw on a winning smile and get on with your day!

You Aren't Sure How to Handle Your Social Media Presence Now That You Have a New Job

When you land a new job, you'll more than likely want to share the good news with your network and update your social profiles. Pretty straightforward, right? Yes. But here's something that's not quite as simple: How do you manage your social media presence—and are you even allowed to access your personal accounts—at your new job?

 Try these ideas to address this issue:

1. **Update your profiles with your new information.**
   If you use LinkedIn (which you probably should, as it's arguably the most important professional platform), make sure your privacy settings are set so that your network gets an alert when you add the new job.

2. **Remove references on your social profiles that mentioned that you were looking for a new job.**
   You don't want your new boss to misunderstand and suspect you're already looking.

3. **Find out if your new employer has any specific policies related to how employees use social media at work.**
   They might also offer best practices on how to present yourself. Certainly, these are *your* profiles, but social media can be a powerful tool for professional branding and business building, so check to see if your new employer offers any guidelines or support.

DON'T SHARE ANY INFORMATION related to the clients you're partnering with or projects you're working on before checking with your manager to ensure you're not about to divulge confidential, sensitive, or proprietary information. The last thing you want to do as you kick off a new job is share details that might jeopardize the company's reputation, irk a client, or give competitors access to competitive intelligence. When in doubt, ask before you post.

HERE'S HOW

Now that you're thinking about social media in terms of your career, here are some things to consider before you make any moves on social media.

Think This:

"Am I wasting too many precious hours on my personal accounts?" Starting a new job is a great time to reflect on your social media presence and habits. If so, perhaps try cutting that activity back (if not stopping it entirely) during the workday. Conversely, think about how you might amplify your professional brand and position yourself as a thought leader using your social platforms. By redirecting your energy, you might benefit yourself *and* your new employer.

Say This:

"Do we have a social media policy and, if so, may I review it?"

"How can I best leverage my social media following to support the team or our brand?"

"Can you think of any employees who do a great job promoting our work via social media?"

"Is there anything you want me to stay away from when posting?"

WHAT NEXT?

Assuming your employer gives the green light to social media posting, you're good to go. If you want to take things to the next level career-wise, you could brainstorm topics that may help you further your brand or the company's. If the company is hesitant (or downright oppressive) about employees and social media, you'll need to decide what's next. If you're fine with that stance, great. Otherwise, perhaps you take the lead in helping them understand the potential benefits of a social media presence to the organization.

You Need to Get to Know Your New Coworkers and Boss

Landing an offer and starting a new job is exciting. It's also a little stressful for most people. That awkward period during which you don't know who's who, what's where, or what your boss is *really* like can be tough to navigate. So, how do you survive the awkwardness and get to know your new colleagues without coming across as nervous, nosy, or standoffish?

 Try these ideas to address this issue:

1   **Ask curious questions.**
    While you don't want to come off as a busybody, you can demonstrate your interest in people by asking questions about their lives and their work. And small talk doesn't have to be about the weather! Think up some creative (yet office-appropriate) questions to get the conversation started.

2   **Offer to help.**
    Does your teammate seem overloaded? Ask if you can take something off their plate. Of course, be mindful of your core responsibilities, but lending a hand will provide an instant opportunity to interact.

3   **Find out your boss's preferred communication style.**
    Not everyone likes being interrupted via phone or text. Some hate email. Some have a hard rule that work ends at 5 p.m., so evening chit-chat is a no. Find out proactively, so your outreach efforts are appreciated, not a nuisance.

DON'T GET SUCKED INTO ANY OFFICE GOSSIP OR POLITICS. There's drama in *every* organization. Don't go looking for it, and don't engage with it if someone brings it to you. Your first days and weeks will set the stage for how your supervisor, peers, and clients view you. If you get into immediate cahoots with the gossip spreaders, you could damage your credibility right from the start. Steer clear.

HERE'S HOW Now that you've got the basics, here are specific tips and talking points you can use as you meet and get to know the team.

Think This:	Say This:
"Reaching out to build relationships will help me establish connections and build camaraderie with my coworkers." Even if you're introverted, it's important that you try to learn more about the people you're working with. Strong communication is vital in any organization; you'll be working collaboratively on projects at some point or another. Think of this relationship-building as a key part of your onboarding experience—it's just as important as setting up your payroll information.	"What do you like to do outside of work?" "Who do you really look up to at our company, and why?" "What made you decide to work here?" "Who's the funniest person on our team?" "Can you recommend any good lunch places nearby?"

WHAT NEXT? ⟶

As you become acquainted with your boss and coworkers, try to remember your conversations and the information they've shared. If you know your teammate loves chai latte, grab them one every now and then (or, if you're virtual, send a gift card!). If at first you are struggling to make strong connections, don't give up. Some people take longer to open up than others, and your shared experience working together will likely bring you closer with time. Business is about people. The more you connect with *your* people, the more enjoyable your job will be.

You Need to Ask for More Training on a New Task

Whether you're in a brand-new job or have been at your company for years, sometimes a project comes along that you need additional skills to complete. You might need to get comfortable with a software program, a new machine, or a workflow or process you haven't participated in yet. Who should you approach to get some training, and how should you go about it?

 *Try these ideas to address this issue:*

1 **If you just need quick guidance, ask your manager or a coworker if they'd be willing to help you.**
Any reasonable boss or peer will be happy to show you the ropes. You might be a 30-minute tutorial away from proficiency. Every company does things a bit differently, but your employer should be motivated to get you trained so you can fulfill your job responsibilities.

2 **Investigate upcoming learning opportunities.**
If the company has a training team, ask a trainer for advice on how to get up to speed efficiently.

3 **Ask for more extensive help.**
If it's clear you'll need more immersive training than your company offers, research some cost-efficient training opportunities, then approach your boss with your request to see if the company will pay for all, or at least some, of the fee. Explain how the team and organization will benefit from the investment in your continuing education.

DON'T MAKE IT YOUR BOSS'S RESPONSIBILITY to bring you up to speed if the task you need training on is a baseline requirement for the job (and you, *ahem*, perhaps overstated your proficiency while interviewing). Instead, sleuth out a *YouTube* video, an online course, or a library book that'll help you refresh or advance your knowledge of the thing you were expected to know in the first place.

HERE'S HOW Here are a few additional tips and talking points to guide you as you reach out for help.

Think This:

"It's OK to ask for help." While you may worry that, by asking for training, your manager will second-guess your competence, these concerns are likely unfounded. In fact, part of a boss's job is to ensure that team members have the skills, support, and motivation they need to succeed. Remind yourself that's how *their* success is measured, so managers have every incentive to make sure you're prepared to deliver your absolute best work. Ease your mind and boost your confidence by asking for help.

Say This:

Colleague: "You're a whiz with this software's advanced features. Would you have a moment this week to show me how to customize the interface?"

Trainer: "Are there any sessions coming up that'll help me understand our safety protocols? May I sign up?"

Boss: "This supply chain analytics course will help me to better understand the data we need to predict demand faster and more accurately. If the company covers the cost of this course for me, I anticipate we'll see quick improvements in order fulfillment!"

WHAT NEXT?

Once you get the training, express your gratitude. If a peer or company trainer helped you learn a task, offer to buy lunch (or send them a gift card). If your boss approved some training, be sure to say thanks. More importantly, show them that you're applying what you learned to better the organization. If you've taken training but still find yourself struggling, don't beat yourself up. We all learn in different ways. Instead, ask your boss for a mentor or ongoing coaching to help position you for success.

You Discover Your Job Is Nothing Like Described in the Interview

You make it through several rounds of interviews and land what seems like an incredible new job. But as you settle in, you begin to suspect something's not quite right. Perhaps you signed on to oversee the firm's marketing campaigns only to find yourself buried in accounting spreadsheets. Or maybe you expected to manage a team and discover you actually have no direct reports. What do you do if you suddenly feel that you may be the victim of a career bait and switch?

 Try these ideas to address this issue:

1   **Give it a minute.**
    While you don't want to get stuck in a job that's not aligned with your goals, resist making any rash decisions. A slow or strange start may not be reflective of the overall job.

2   **Talk to your manager.**
    If it's obvious there's a disconnect, ask for a meeting. Bring the job description you applied for and a list of tasks you've been managing to the conversation. Spell out your concerns calmly and work to collaboratively refine the scope of the role.

3   **Figure out if there are any job(s) at your new organization better aligned with your skill set and expectations.**
    If needed, ask if you might shift over to that team. If you like the company, but not the job (and revising your job description doesn't seem to be an option), it can't hurt to ask.

DON'T JUST SIT AROUND HOPING THINGS WILL GET BETTER. Even if you really like the organization and your coworkers, if you find yourself in a job that's been miscategorized, don't expect someone else to fix the situation for you. You'll not only waste time doing work you don't love; your silence may indicate tacit acceptance of the situation. Worse, the longer you stay in the wrong job, the harder it could become to switch back into something more in line with your skills and experience.

HERE'S HOW These things to think about and suggested scripts can help you work through the current situation and avoid similar disappointment down the road.

Think This:

"I shouldn't waste a lot of time thinking about who's to blame for this discrepancy." The current hiring manager may not have even written the job description. And, in some companies, the process of revising them is a painstaking bureaucratic undertaking. As you work toward a solution, keep your attention on doing your best work. You can also think about whether there are questions you could ask during your next interview phase to be sure this doesn't happen to you again.

Say This:

"It seems the requirements of the job are different than those we discussed at the interview. Could we meet to ensure I'm clear on expectations?"

"Here's the job description and here's what I've been working on. When can I expect to dig into projects that align with this?"

"I accepted the job in large part for the opportunity to do _____. Has something changed?"

WHAT NEXT?

If you and your boss reach an agreement on the true nature of your job, great. Roll up your sleeves and get down to business. If you just don't see it working out, you can decide what's next. Do you stay at the company and wait for it to be resolved? Or do you cut your losses and leave now? If you turned down another role for this one (or had other opportunities in progress), check in with your recruiter or point person. Who knows? It may not be too late to be considered!

You Want to Understand How to Define "Success" at Your New Job

Defining success is tricky—depending on the industry and company, it can be done via a mixture of objective and subjective measures. Oddly, some companies aren't always clear and transparent about how they'll determine whether you're doing well in your role. But this is information you need right from the start to be sure you're working toward the same goal. So how can you ensure you get this info, stat?

 Try these ideas to address this issue:

1 Ask about goals.
It's in your best interest to quickly determine how your boss (and the company) defines success for your role, and how and when it will be measured. In your first one-on-one meeting with your manager, ask this question: "What specific performance goals do you have for me?"

2 Be sure expectations are clear.
Make sure the metrics laid out are measurable and that the evaluation period is finite.

3 Find out if and how success is rewarded.
Are there quarterly or annual bonuses? Is there a set career progression for high performers? Awards?

4 See who's involved.
Ask if others besides your boss will be evaluating your success—peers, clients, self-assessment, etc.

5 Make your own metrics.
If no metrics exist, ask your manager if you might propose your own or create some together.

DON'T RELY ON WHAT SO-AND-SO TOLD YOU AS YOU WERE INTERVIEWING or information you heard second-hand from a colleague or whatever you are assuming "success" should be. What happens if so-and-so was mistaken and now you're focusing on the wrong priorities? Scenarios like this could get messy for you and, in the worst case, jeopardize your job. Don't guess—ask for this information directly, and be sure you get it in writing.

HERE'S HOW Here are a few additional things to think about and say as you work to gain clarity.

Think This:	**Say This:**
"I'm not being a nuisance, a brownnoser, or a stickler for rules by asking how success will be measured." By having agreed-upon expectations and tangible metrics, you'll be able to focus on the areas that matter the most to your manager and the company, prioritize and schedule your time strategically, and—importantly—maximize your impact, for both the organization and your career.	"What are the three most important aspects of my job?" "May I see a copy of the form you'll use when completing my annual performance review?" "Aside from the quantifiable metrics, what qualitative measures do you use in evaluating my performance?" "How will you alert me if you feel I'm falling behind or not achieving my core goals?"

WHAT NEXT?

If you can clarify things with your employer, fantastic. Thank your boss for outlining your path to success and dig in! If you're experiencing pushback—or general fuzziness regarding your role—schedule a meeting with HR. It's crucial that you understand expectations so that you may thrive in your role.

You Need to Set Work-Life Boundaries

You're committed to working hard in your job, but feel equally committed to ensuring you've got something left in the tank for your family, friends, and outside activities. Hopefully, your company (and boss) supports work-life balance. Even if they do, though, you could find yourself in situations where you need to set or remind others of your boundaries. How can you do this, especially when you're new?

 Try these ideas to address this issue:

1. **Know that everyone deserves to have a workload that's manageable.**
   This is true whether you're a rookie or veteran employee.

2. **Get clear on what's expected.**
   You don't want to push back on something that's a basic requirement of the job. Read the fine print before speaking up.

3. **Establish open lines of communication with your boss.**
   This is always good advice, but it will be especially helpful if you need to clarify a boundary or politely say no to an unreasonable request.

4. **Choose your timing (and words) thoughtfully.**
   It's important to advocate for your needs, but you can still be smart about how and when you make your request.

5. **Create a routine for yourself, make people aware of it, and try to stick with it.**
   If everyone knows you coach youth hockey every Thursday after work, they probably won't book you into an end-of-day meeting.

DON'T LET A BAD SITUATION FESTER. If it seems like finding a healthy work-life balance may be challenging or impossible in your new environment, address it quickly with your boss—otherwise, you'll end up feeling burned out and resentful. If you can't work out a good solution to the problem with your manager, don't stay in the job just because you fear how it might look on your resume.

HERE'S HOW

Now that you've got the basics down, here are a few things to consider—and say—as you work to achieve work-life balance.

Think This:

"My work-life balance is an ongoing journey, not a destination." Your schedule will experience ebbs and flows depending on work projects in progress, family demands, etc. If you expect perfect balance every day, you'll likely be disappointed when things inevitably tilt one way or another. Whenever your attention is pulled too far in one direction, remind yourself of your goals and adjust as needed.

Say This:

"I need to spend time with family after work. Are you okay if I don't check my email after 6 p.m.?"

"I notice people tend to work through lunch here. I'm at my best if I take a quick lunch break, though. Is that acceptable to you?"

"That was an intense project! I'd like to spend tomorrow getting caught up on email and catching my breath, okay?"

WHAT NEXT?

If you're successful in getting your point across that you need a bit more balance, well done. Now be sure to give your employer your absolute best during the hours you're focused on work. If you find that your manager (or company leadership overall) just doesn't recognize the value of rest or a sane schedule in general, you can either make it your mission to help them see the light...or make it your mission to move on to a company that will.

You Want to Fit In with the Company Culture

No matter how excited you are to start a new job, those early days of feeling like an awkward newcomer can be tough. And if you're like many new hires, you'll probably find that settling into the rhythm of your day-to-day responsibilities isn't the hardest part—it's understanding and assimilating with your new team and organization. How can you fit into a new company culture efficiently?

 Try these ideas to address this issue:

1. **Introduce yourself to everyone ASAP.**
   Strive to remember their names and an interesting detail or two about them. While your skills and experience were key to your being hired, success in business is about relationships. The more quickly you build strong ones, the better.

2. **Observe and listen.**
   Figure out the stuff that's not in the employee manual. How and when do your coworkers interact? Who are the go-to people, the high performers, the gossips? How are decisions made?

3. **Ask questions.**
   Certainly, be mindful that your colleagues also have jobs to do, but don't be afraid to raise your hand as you navigate those first weeks on the job.

4. **Learn the lingo.**
   Every company has its own buzzwords, phrases, acronyms (oh, the acronyms), and nuances. The faster you learn them, the more confident you'll feel.

DON'T BE ANYTHING OTHER THAN YOUR AUTHENTIC SELF. No one wants to work with a phony, and, assuming you've scored a good boss, they'll encourage and celebrate everyone's personalities. With luck, you already made some assessments while interviewing as to how well the culture aligns with your values and style. So, showing up as your true self should be pretty doable. And if it's not? It may be time to rethink your decision.

✓ **HERE'S HOW** If you're still worried about fitting in with the new company culture, here's something to consider—and some talking points to help ease the transition.

Think This:

"I will just be myself." Without a doubt, your manager chose you for the job partly because they felt you'd fit in well with the team already in place. So rather than worry about how you're fitting in, just focus on being yourself and making connections with the people around you. Think about all the value you're bringing to the position, and let your good work and winning personality speak for themselves!

Say This:

"What adjectives would you use to describe our team?"

"When you hired me, how did you see me fitting in with the team?"

"What makes you proud about working for this company?"

"What about this company (or our team) would you like to change?"

"When you started your job here, are there specific things you did that helped you assimilate quickly?"

WHAT NEXT? ⟶

If you hit the ground running and have made friends already, congratulations! If you're still feeling awkward after your first few weeks, try not to read too much into it, especially if your entire team is remote. Settling into a new environment takes time, especially if you're not face-to-face. If you're still not finding your groove with the team or company after a few months, ask your manager or a friendly coworker for advice on how to best get your footing. Great relationships take time, work ones included!

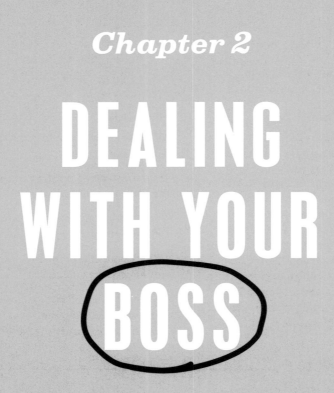

Chapter 2

DEALING WITH YOUR BOSS

When you have a great relationship with your manager, life is a whole lot easier. Great bosses ensure that you feel supported yet challenged, prioritize your growth and development, and leave you without a doubt that their door is *always* open. But even the strongest and most enviable boss-employee relationships come with at least occasional headaches, misunderstandings, or frustrations. We all say things we wish we hadn't, have hang-ups and particularities, and manage stressors on and off the job. We also have varying communication styles, values, goals, and expectations.

Given all these factors (and more!), it should come as no surprise when you run into an issue with your manager that needs to be ironed out. It might be something relatively straightforward: Maybe you need their input on a project, yet they're chronically unavailable, or they assign a task that you're just too busy to take on.

It could, however, be something more serious or high stakes that needs to be addressed and resolved before it damages your health, sanity, professional integrity, or employment. What are you to do if, for example, your manager cannot control their explosive temper?

In this chapter, you'll learn how to calmly raise issues, confidently advocate for your needs, sidestep potential pitfalls, respond if things don't go as planned, and elevate the matter if necessary. These strategies are designed to help you survive the immediate situation with your boss and, with luck, enable you to build or restore a solid working relationship.

You Don't Agree with a Decision Your Boss Made

No two people get along with one another 100 percent of the time. Despite how normal a situation this is, however, discord at work can really ratchet up your anxiety, especially if you're conflict averse by nature. Your boss might have made a small decision that is really affecting your day-to-day life, or they might have implemented a big-picture change that makes you question the company's direction. So what should you do if your manager makes a decision that you oppose?

 Try these ideas to address this issue:

1 **Pick the right time.**
Ideally, you've built up a solid relationship with your manager and the lines of communication are open. Even if that's the case, resist the urge to blurt out your opinion in the heat of the moment. You'll want to be thoughtful in how and when you voice your dissent.

2 **Separate the issue from the person.**
If, say, your manager announces they're giving the primo client account to your peer versus you (and you totally deserve it!), this doesn't automatically make them a horrible person. It's the decision that you think stinks.

3 **Strive to understand your boss's point of view.**
Before jumping to conclusions, try asking a few questions to better understand the rationale behind the decision.

4 **Suggest an alternative.**
If you disagree, don't just gripe; share a constructive idea around what might work better. (And be ready to sell it!)

DON'T VENT AND GOSSIP TO YOUR COWORKERS ABOUT A DECISION YOUR BOSS HAS MADE. Sure, that may be all you need—a listening ear, a good cry, or confirmation that your assessment of the situation has merit. But it's important to respect yourself and your boss enough to say your piece directly to your boss. Resist the urge to talk about your feelings behind their back. Even if it's a difficult conversation, having it directly with your manager is the better choice.

HERE'S HOW

Consider these ideas and conversation starters as you determine how you'll proceed.

Think This:

"This difficult conversation could lead to great things." Finding the gumption to refute a boss's decision may seem daunting, but it can actually benefit you in many ways. Done well, advocating for yourself, your needs, or your team could reap many rewards. It's an opportunity to build confidence, demonstrate your communication skills, and affirm your natural leadership—all of which may help you to advance your career more quickly than those who choose to stew silently.

Say This:

"I was thinking more about your decision. Can we discuss the consequences it may have on my job?"

"When can we discuss your plan to reorganize sales territories?"

"Could you please outline for me how you came to the decision?"

"Consolidating our East Coast territory is smart. However, I fear the proposed changes will compromise the South, and here's why."

WHAT NEXT?

If your manager agrees that your concerns are justified and your ideas have merit, great! If, however, your boss refuses to even consider your point of view, you'll need to determine your next move. If the decision involves something serious, you may need to elevate the issue to your boss's boss or Human Resources. (Or, at worst, consider a new job.) But make this your last resort. Do everything you can to voice your opinion respectfully directly to your boss and find an agreeable outcome.

You Don't Agree with Your Annual Performance Assessment

In a perfect world, you won't get all the way to your annual review and learn something shocking about the way in which your performance has been evaluated. Assuming your manager's been, well, *managing* you all year, you should have had time to fix any performance issues prior to your annual assessment. But life's imperfect, and sometimes that shows up in the form of a review you disagree with. What then?

 *Try these ideas to address this issue:*

1   Get clarification.
Make sure you understand where your manager is coming from with the mark(s) you've been given and the criteria they used for the evaluation.

2   Ask for supporting examples.
This is especially important if your boss is using subjective metrics (e.g., "teamwork" or "attitude") versus objective data.

3   Create a rebuttal.
If you still disagree, draft an email or talking points outlining what you disagree with, share any data that supports your argument, and request a meeting to discuss further.

4   If needed, go to Human Resources.
Obviously, this will elevate the situation, so make sure you're prepared for any intensity that may follow. But if you're passionate about the issue and feel you're not being heard, this may be your best option.

DON'T LOSE YOUR COOL! No matter how upset you are or how vehemently you disagree with your manager's assessment of your performance, you probably won't achieve a positive outcome if you allow your emotions to get the best of you. And you don't have to sign the review on the spot either. If you need time to simmer down, think about things, and make decisions with a clear head, let your manager know that you'd like to digest the review more thoroughly and request reconvening within the next couple of days.

HERE'S HOW   Once you've got the gist of how to proceed when your review goes sideways (and how not to), here's how to fine-tune your mindset and your response.

Think This:

"One less-than-stellar review doesn't sink a whole career." Keep things in perspective and do what you can to right the ship, especially if any parts of the review do have merit. Either way, by advocating for yourself—no matter the outcome—you may very well show your employer that you're not a wallflower and show yourself that, done well, speaking up can be quite liberating and effective.

Say This:

"If I'm hearing you correctly, you're saying _____, correct?"

"Can you give me a few examples so I may better understand what led you to give me this mark?"

"I suspect you didn't factor in my work with [important project] as you assessed my performance. Could we discuss this?"

"I'm admittedly a bit taken aback and would prefer talking after I think this through. Can we reconvene tomorrow?"

WHAT NEXT? ⟶

If you're successful in convincing your manager to revisit your performance review, congratulate yourself for standing up for yourself and remember to take any constructive criticism to heart. If, in spite of your efforts, your boss won't budge, you'll need to decide if you'll press the issue further by going to Human Resources. If that feels too difficult, you can either let things go, or consider finding a new employer.

Your Boss Seems to Be Unavailable Whenever You Need Support

Good bosses are inclusive, uplifting, and available to their teams. They're also human—and most of them are busy humans with piles of work on their plates nearly all the time. Some managers are masters at juggling these constant demands. But if "Sorry, I just don't have time for you today" becomes a regular response, how can you get the guidance you need?

 **Try these ideas to address this issue:**

1. **Study their habits.**
   You can't control their availability, but you can likely figure out their patterns to see if you can grab them in a free moment. So, rather than mope about being ignored, try catching them for a quick chat when they head to the cafeteria for their latte fix.

2. **Take initiative.**
   This one's simple: Don't wait for an invite. Instead, create a calendar invite for a regular one-on-one. If your manager is swamped, be realistic with suggested frequency, but it's perfectly reasonable to expect at least periodic face time.

3. **Come prepared.**
   Enter that meeting with an agenda in hand and put the most timely and important action items at the top.

4. **Flip the script.**
   Ask your boss how you might lighten their load. Who knows? If you free up time on their calendar, they may be willing to use it for you!

DON'T START SLACKING OFF OR ACTING PASSIVE-AGGRESSIVELY. If your work output suffers, you're only negatively impacting your own performance. Also, it's usually not a good idea to immediately go over your boss's head to complain about the situation. Be sure you've given your boss a fair opportunity to course-correct using the tips in this section.

HERE'S HOW

Consider these ideas and discussion starters if you plan to bring up the topic with your manager.

Think This:

"I will not take this personally." Most likely, this isn't about you or your worthiness of support. It's far more likely that your manager also lacks support, is dealing with unrealistic demands, or just isn't great at time management. They could be going through personal issues that you don't know about. No matter what's driving their unavailability, try to take your hurt feelings out of the equation as you drum up a solution or workaround.

Say This:

"I know you've got a lot on your plate, but I could really use some support."

"Given your demands, do you think [other employee] would be a good alternative resource for feedback?"

"I want to knock it out of the park with this project. May I set up a weekly meeting to touch base on my progress?"

"Your schedule seems crazy right now. How can I help free up some time for you?"

WHAT NEXT?

If you can get to a spot where you feel adequately supported by your boss and/or your colleagues, fantastic. It may require a bit more effort or creativity on your part, but it'll be worth it, both sanity- and career-wise. But if, after giving it your all, you still fear your manager's chronic unavailability will make it hard for you to succeed, you may want to explore other departments (or even a new company) to call home. At that point, your HR department might be a helpful resource.

You Are Too Busy to Take On a Newly Assigned Project

Ask any working professional, and they'll probably say they'd rather be busy than bored. The days go by faster, you feel a sense of purpose, and you generally learn and grow more when you've got a lot going on workwise. But there's a fine line between "busy" and "overloaded," and it can be pretty daunting when your boss assigns that one extra project that takes you across the line. How can you handle this tricky situation?

 Try these ideas to address this issue:

1 **Before sounding the alarm, quickly assess the big picture.**
Try to objectively evaluate why you're feeling overwhelmed. Is it *just* work stuff, or are personal stressors compounding things? Do you lack skills that you need to be successful? Might you have a time management issue?

2 **Be transparent.**
There's a pretty good chance your boss has no clue how you're feeling and will genuinely want to fix things, so don't be afraid to speak up.

3 **Be strategic.**
Propose an alternate solution that adjusts a deadline or part of a project. You could also write down all of your projects and ask your boss to help you organize your time.

DON'T KEEP SAYING YES FOR FEAR YOU'LL DISAPPOINT YOUR MANAGER. The reality is that you're far more likely to fall out of favor if you overpromise and underdeliver (especially if it's an important project) than if you raise your hand and ask for support—in a direct and solution-focused manner. Even if you're a warrior when it comes to workload, you don't need to say yes every time when you're struggling.

HERE'S HOW Now that you know what to do and what to steer clear of, here's how to reframe your thoughts and prepare what you'll say.

Think This:

"If I have the courage to be vulnerable, people can really know me and, in this case, help me." Asking for help takes courage, especially when you feel vulnerable. We are all our own worst critics, and, in situations like this, you may convince yourself that speaking up will make you look weak or incompetent. But the real strength lies in knowing your limits and getting help when you need it.

Say This:

"It's really important to me that I deliver my best work. I'm worried that I won't be able to with this project, and here's why."

"I'll be glad to tackle this project, but I'm concerned it will pull me away from [other project]. What would you suggest I do?"

"Here are all the projects I'm working on right now. Could you help me prioritize or delegate?"

WHAT NEXT?

If your manager agrees to help, great! Thank them, then confirm the conversation via email, so the decisions you made together are in writing. If they don't respond with any empathy or flexibility, think about enlisting peers on your own, asking your family to help free up some time, or—if this happens regularly—seeking a more manageable job. Life's too short to be spent with employers that expect their employees to bear crushing workloads.

Your Boss Keeps Asking You to Do Things Outside of Your Job Scope

Everyone is assigned a bit of "etcetera" from time to time. Your boss may need your help on an urgent project, ask you to do some research, or want you to take on some copying/filing/lunch ordering—even if this isn't your actual job. And for these occasional requests, it's smart to demonstrate flexibility and say yes. But what if your manager continually assigns you work that's decidedly not in your job description?

 Try these ideas to address this issue:

1 **Politely ask your manager to sit down and review your job description.**
If the requests are never-ending—and it's getting old fast—you'll be wise to set some boundaries. They may not even realize they're asking you to do things that are outside of your job scope. This meeting is an opportunity for you to collaboratively align expectations.

2 **Make a list of what you're working on at the moment.**
And then ask if you should continue to focus on these priorities or on the thing they have asked you to do.

3 **Put things in perspective for your boss.**
Say they ask you to make copies for every meeting, even though you're a manager. Try saying something like "I'm glad to help, but I wonder if I should instead use my time to work through our urgent client issue?"

4 **Ask for a raise.**
If the work you're regularly being asked to do is well above your pay grade, you should be paid for doing it.

DON'T UTTER THIS PHRASE: "THAT'S NOT MY JOB." It's universally despised and could make you look difficult or arrogant. Also, keep in mind that most job descriptions come with a little catch-all phrase like "Additional duties as required." There are many ways to try to address the situation while still being a team player and a positive colleague, so don't resort to petty responses.

HERE'S HOW Now that you understand how to approach your boss, here are a few more tips to help you navigate the situation.

Think This:

"I need to keep an open mind." Depending on the circumstance, there may be times when it'd be quite reasonable for you to say no, but you should actually consider saying yes. For instance, maybe it's an unusual all-hands-on-deck period at work and your support is critical. Try mentally reframing the situation and, rather than being annoyed, view it as an opportunity to gain new skills, build deeper relationships with coworkers, or be the one who saved the day for everyone!

Say This:

"That's not really in my wheelhouse. May I suggest we get [coworker] involved?"

"Based on recent assignments, it seems the scope of my job may be changing. Could we meet to discuss potentially shifting my role (and/or compensation)?"

"Part of the reason I joined the team was to have opportunity to rebrand the organization. May I get back to this work soon?"

WHAT NEXT?

If your manager is receptive to your request to spend more time on your core responsibilities—or revise your role and compensation accordingly—express your appreciation, then strive to be flexible if occasional one-off requests come your way. If, however, it seems clear that the job just isn't going to be what you signed up for, think hard about how this might impact your career going forward—and decide if you need an exit strategy.

You Need to Discuss a Major Health Issue with Your Boss

With luck, you work for a company that values and promotes compassion, honesty, and transparency, so you feel safe to share ideas and can communicate openly and freely with your manager and peers. Still, if you have or develop a major health issue, it can be difficult to share the news, even if you work in an incredibly supportive environment. What's the best way to disclose this information—or should you keep it to yourself?

 Try these ideas to address this issue:

1 **Alert your boss.**
If your illness will impact your work, you should communicate your condition constructively and concisely.

2 **Make sure you understand your options—and your rights.**
If you're in the US, pay particular attention to protections offered by the Family and Medical Leave Act (FMLA) and Americans with Disabilities Act (ADA), especially if you'll need time off for treatment or recovery.

3 **Keep it general.**
You're under no obligation to provide your employer the nitty-gritty details. Share what you need to, and no more.

4 **Ask for what you need.**
While your boss will likely be empathetic, don't count on them to know how to accommodate you. Be sure to spell out what changes are necessary to help you get through this period of time.

5 **Do your part.**
Assuming your manager provides the flexibility and support you seek, be sure to hold up your end of the deal as best you can.

DON'T TRY TO POWER THROUGH A SIGNIFICANT HEALTH ISSUE ALONE OR UNDETECTED BY YOUR EMPLOYER. Even if you take great pride in never taking sick days, your stoicism could work against you, especially if you can't keep up with your workload or perform to your expected level through an illness. Remember that acting like nothing is wrong will leave people to draw their own conclusions from what they observe. If you cannot disguise that something is amiss, it's best to proactively control the message.

HERE'S HOW Here are a few additional thoughts and discussion points to use as you firm up if and how you will proceed.

Think This:

"My health comes first." While it's understandable to worry about your job (especially if it's providing health insurance), mentally prioritize getting yourself back to a healthy state. It's not selfish, weak, or needy to have to change your work responsibilities while you tackle a health issue. Focus on getting well, and reassure yourself that you'll return to giving 100 percent to your job when you are able to.

Say This:

"I've been diagnosed with cancer and need treatment. Here are my upcoming appointment times, and what I'll need from you if you're amenable."

"My doctor has suggested that a reduced work schedule will likely alleviate my symptoms. May I share some ideas on how this might work?"

"I'll be unable to work for eight weeks. My leave will be covered under FMLA, correct?"

WHAT NEXT? ⟶

Assuming your employer is supportive of your situation, ask for confirmation of the agreement in writing, then allow yourself to prioritize what truly matters right now—your health. If you encounter any hassles as you disclose or afterward, start documenting everything and request a meeting with Human Resources, ASAP. You may have certain legal rights that you should be sure you're receiving. If your employer is still unsupportive, consider a move to a company that will value your professional skills *and* your health.

Your Boss Asks You to Do Something Unethical

You're humming along, doing great work, when your boss asks you to do something that just doesn't feel right. Maybe they want you to intentionally mislead a client, fudge the numbers on a report, or cover for something they've done that's well outside of company policy. At worst, you may be asked to do something that's not just unethical, but illegal. If you find yourself in this spot, how on earth do you respond?

 *Try these ideas to address this issue:*

1 **Ask for clarification.**
Did you hear correctly? Is there a chance you've misunderstood what's being asked of you? Get clear before you react.

2 **Evaluate the pros and cons.**
There's no doubt that the stakes are high no matter how you respond to the request. Lead with your values as you consider how your answer may impact your reputation, your well-being, and your employment.

3 **Be respectful, but clear.**
Assuming you plan to push back on the request, try doing so in a way that allows your boss to save face while still asserting your position. For example, "I know you would never ask me to do something that might be considered bribery. To be on the safe side, I'll plan to do [more ethical thing] instead, ok?"

4 **Protect yourself.**
Get as much in writing as possible so that, if things go sideways or you face punishment, you have documentation that clears your good name.

DON'T IGNORE A STRONG GUT FEELING. If, after clarifying the request and pondering pros and cons, you're *still* feeling like something's just not right, guess what? Something's probably not right. While your brain might be trying to tell you, "Oh, I'm sure it's not such a big deal," if your palms are sweaty, your stomach is flip-flopping, or your jaw is like a steel clamp, this could very well be your body screaming, "Warning!"

HERE'S HOW Once you're square on the basics, here are a few things to contemplate and say as you navigate this very tricky situation.

Think This:

"I'm going to stay true to my values." This, above all, should be your guiding mantra as you work out how you're going to proceed in this—and any—difficult workplace situation. The right decision is not always the easy decision. It could come with consequences like bullying, retaliation, or even termination of your job. But you stand to lose much more if you go along with a clearly unethical request.

Say This:

"Am I missing something or are you asking me to forge the client's signature on this contract?"

"I fear we both may get into hot water if I agree to that. How about we do _____ instead, so we can be sure to avoid violating the law?"

"It's important to me to always be a fair and ethical manager. I'm afraid what you've asked me to do would compromise my values and my reputation. I'm sorry, but I can't do that."

WHAT NEXT?

Once you've made up your mind and responded to your boss's request, stand firm. You may get a bit of pushback or grumbling at first, especially if you've decided to decline. But assuming you've made your decision thoughtfully, be confident it's the right one. And if the pushback continues—or worse, accelerates—get some advice from HR or an employment attorney and/or resign.

Your Boss Credits Someone Else for Work You Did

Most workers want pretty much the same thing: to feel appreciated for their contributions at work. Whether that's in the form of big fanfare, quiet thanks, or something in between, it just feels good to be credited for a job well done. Unfortunately, sometimes your manager overlooks your achievements. Or worse, they give credit to someone else for your efforts or ideas. What then?

 Try these ideas to address this issue:

1 Ask yourself how often it's happened.
If it's an occasional oversight, you probably don't need to say or do anything. But if it's a chronic issue—or something really important to you— say something.

2 Have a private conversation with your boss.
This could be an honest mistake. Cool down, then ask your manager if they'd not realized your involvement in the project when they credited your colleague.

3 Speak up *ever so casually* in meetings.
A simple, "When I came up with the original idea…" will let people know you're the brains behind the operation without coming across as that exhausting coworker who needs constant accolades.

4 Document your work.
Whether you do so privately or via emails to your boss or peers, track and communicate your contributions so there's no confusion over your efforts.

5 Be generous in crediting others for *their* work.
By acknowledging your colleagues, you may find the law of reciprocity works in your favor.

DON'T SPEND A TON OF TIME AND ENERGY LOOKING FOR YOUR BOSS OR COLLEAGUES TO SALUTE EVERY LITTLE WIN YOU DELIVER. Yes, it's very nice to be recognized for your hard work and achievements. And, yes, if you find yourself falling through the cracks regularly, you'll want to address it. But don't let a lack of accolades prevent you from showing up every day and doing great work.

HERE'S HOW Now that you understand what to do and what to avoid, here are some additional considerations and ideas to help you move forward.

Think This:	Say This:
"Regularly letting my hard work go unnoticed could affect my career." While it's generally great to be humble, if your boss consistently commends the wrong person for the work you're contributing, you could be overlooked for raises or promotions if the powers that be aren't aware of your amazing work. It's not selfish to take your credit where and when it's due!	"Maria really appreciated you congratulating her on the new client. When I recommended that she reach out to my contact there, I had a hunch it would be a great fit for our firm!" "I know your schedule is tight right now, so I'll plan to share updates on my progress every Friday via email, okay?" "Jamal really took charge when I outlined how he could best proceed with the new product implementation. Thanks so much for noticing."

WHAT NEXT?

If your efforts are successful—and your boss starts delivering credit where credit is due—quietly pat yourself on the back and keep right on slaying it in your job while recognizing others who do the same. If your manager continues to pass credit on to others (or worse, takes credit for your work themselves), keep delivering amazing work as you plan how you can gain visibility in this job—or plan your move to the next one.

Your Boss Puts You on the Spot During a Meeting

You're coasting through a team meeting when, out of nowhere, your manager asks you to explain or weigh in on something that you know nothing—or very little—about. You gulp, you squirm, your palms start to sweat. How can you come up with something intelligent to contribute, and fast?

 Try these ideas to address this issue:

1. **Buy yourself some time.**
   Try asking this: "I think what you're asking is ____, correct?" In other words, make sure you understand what your boss is asking, while giving yourself a moment to collect your thoughts.

2. **Share whatever you do know on the topic.**
   Then offer to do a bit of research and report back.

3. **Try crowdsourcing the answer.**
   Maybe someone in the room has some input or expertise. Try asking the group, "Does anyone else have thoughts on this?"

4. **Insert the line, "From my limited perspective..." before you share your thoughts.**
   This tells your manager and the group that you're not speaking as an expert but will be glad to share what you know.

DON'T PRESENT ANYTHING AS FACT IF YOU HAVE LITTLE EXPERTISE ON THE TOPIC YOUR BOSS HAS JUST ASKED YOU TO WEIGH IN ON. At best, you could accidently misinform people, and at worst, a colleague could call you out publicly on your incorrect response. It's better to ask for more time to research than to wing it—and regret it.

HERE'S HOW
Once you're clear on how to react if you're put on the spot, consider these additional tips as you fine-tune your internal reaction and your actual response.

Think This:

"My manager probably doesn't even realize that they're putting me in the hot seat." Sure, it's possible that they do, but rather than assuming that your boss is out to get you, consider that it may be innocent; they may just be genuinely interested in your opinion. Then try to look on the bright side. As uncomfortable as the moment may feel, refining your ability to think on your feet can be really beneficial across many aspects of your career.

Say This:

"Wow, that's a great question. Can I do some digging and share my findings with the group via email tomorrow?"

"I'll offer my quick opinion now, and then, if okay with everyone, I'll share a more detailed response after the meeting."

If the environment is casual, try a joke like: "That question is next level. Can I phone a friend?"

WHAT NEXT?

Assuming it was unusual for your boss to catch you off guard, take the lesson from the experience and move forward into future meetings with your newfound best practices in mind. If, however, you feel that your boss is doing this repeatedly and on purpose, you may wish to calmly approach them to discuss your observations. See if you can't agree on a better method going forward, such as your boss giving you a heads-up about these sorts of questions ahead of the meeting.

You Cry in a Meeting with Your Boss

You're in a tough discussion with your manager when you feel it coming. The lump forms in your throat, your eyes start to twitch, and, before you know it, the tears are falling. Most people try hard to avoid crying in the office, especially in front of the boss. But for the sheer number of hours we spend at work, it's bound to happen from time to time. What should you do when and if the weeping begins?

 Try these ideas to address this issue:

1. **Remember that you are a human with emotions, and we all need a good cry sometimes.**
   That said, if you don't want to show that level of emotion in the workplace, try these following steps.

2. **Take a few deep breaths.**
   It will alert your parasympathetic nervous system that your body's ready to calm down.

3. **Try thinking about something pleasant or even hilarious.**
   (It's worth a shot.)

4. **Pinch yourself gently.**
   Studies show that pinching your nose or the skin between your thumb and pointer finger can ebb the flow of tears fast.

5. **Step out of the room for a few moments.**
   If you need a moment to collect yourself, ask to be excused so that you may regroup. Then come back when you're ready to resume the conversation.

HERE'S HOW Beyond the basic dos and don'ts, use these tips as you move forward.

Think This:	Say This:
"Letting an occasional tear slip at the office isn't going to sink my career." Don't beat yourself up for showing emotion when you're mad, frustrated, sad, or overwhelmed. The truth is that some people just cry more easily than others—and that may be you. You might want to reflect on how the situation became so emotionally charged to see if there's anything you can do in the future to address issues before they reach that level.	"I am dealing with a difficult situation right now and I'd appreciate it if you'd give me a bit of space to process it." "I'm crying because this is really important to me, and I want to make sure we succeed." "I come from a family of big criers. I'm frustrated right now and hoping you'll hear me out on how I think we should proceed."

WHAT NEXT?

If your manager is invested in your well-being and success, chances are your tears won't rattle them, and they'll be understanding and move on. If, however, you detect that the company culture or your manager's expectations are destined to prompt regular tears (and not the happy kind) or limit your chances for success, it may be time to find an employer that's a better fit.

Your Boss Is a Micromanager

Anyone who's ever reported to a micromanager will surely tell you this: Being under the thumb of an inflexible, hypercontrolling boss can be a truly soul-crushing experience, and one that creates piles of anxiety and resentment for everyone involved. Having someone look over your shoulder all the time prevents you from building confidence and growing professionally. Is there anything you can do to take back some control from a boss who nitpicks everything?

 Try these ideas to address this issue:

1 Beat them at their own game.
Once you figure out how your boss operates, you may be able to guess what they'll want next or how they'll expect an assignment to be done. Remember that info and get the assignment completed (to your manager's standards) before they even ask.

2 Ask others for input.
If your boss has been at the company for a while, you can bet there are others who have had to figure out how to survive their ways. Find them, fast.

3 Ask to take the lead.
Request an opportunity to demonstrate your skills and reliability. And assuming you are successful once, you might find less micromanaging on future assignments.

4 Praise them when you get some freedom.
Humans like being recognized, so anytime your boss gives you a bit of autonomy, let them know that you appreciate it.

DON'T TORMENT A MICROMANAGER OUT OF SPITE (e.g., saying things like "I skipped a few steps, but I'm sure *everything will be fine*"). Also, don't assume they're acting this way just to be annoying. Best-case scenario, your manager wants things a certain way because that's what the company needs to be successful.

HERE'S HOW
Shift your thinking and how you respond to your micromanaging boss to preserve your sanity and, with luck, gain more agency in your work.

Think This:

"Chances are, this person has a lot going on under the surface—whether it's a strong sense of perfectionism or a need to be in control." Practicing empathy can help you gain perspective on the situation—you might see that they're just trying to be sure the department produces top-notch work. Also, know that some bosses' micromanaging doesn't have anything to do with the quality of your work—they may request changes *anytime* they review *anything*.

Say This:

"I emailed you a detailed progress report and will update you on the project weekly. Will that be helpful?"

"I know you haven't seen me design in AutoCAD before, but I'm quite proficient. May I share any work samples?"

"You seem stressed over these deliverables. How can I give you peace of mind that we'll have everything done on time and within budget?"

WHAT NEXT?

While your boss's management style may be deeply ingrained, with patience, tact, and consistently solid performance, you just might build credibility and gain some breathing room. If you make the effort yet still find yourself under the microscope, you may need to get more direct in sharing how their approach is making you feel. (For example, say something like, "I'm feeling a little smothered when you review my work five times before anyone else sees it.") If that fails as well, speak with Human Resources about the challenges you're facing.

Your Boss Is Saying or Doing Inappropriate Things

Inappropriate or offensive behavior in the workplace is a big red flag. Whether the bad behavior is physical, verbal, or emotional, your company should have a plan in place to address it. If your boss, the very person who should be modeling professional behavior, isn't living up to this unspoken professional standard, you'll need to respond. (The same goes for a colleague who's stepping out of line.) How do you deal with this difficult situation?

 Try these ideas to address this issue:

1. **Ask yourself, "How big is the issue?"** Is this a one-time rude moment or consistent actions that make you uncomfortable? (It may require action either way.)

2. **If you feel comfortable doing so, calmly call them out, in real time.** Point out how what they've said or done makes you feel. Sometimes people don't even realize the error of their ways.

3. **Review your company's employee handbook.** See if there is a specific policy against what's going on.

4. **Document everything if the bad behavior continues.** Include evidence that you've asked them to stop.

5. **Report your manager to Human Resources.** If you fear retaliation, consider sharing the information anonymously.

6. **Consult with an experienced employment lawyer.** There are laws that protect you from many forms of harassment.

DON'T GOSSIP ABOUT OR BAD-MOUTH THE PERSON BEHIND THEIR BACK. Yes, this may be hard, especially if the behavior is eroding your well-being or you're fuming mad. But stooping to their level isn't likely to resolve your issue—and could get you in hot water too. Work to demonstrate what professionalism looks like and try to stay focused on your job as you address and work through the issue.

HERE'S HOW Here are a few additional things to think and say as you deal with the person's unacceptable behavior.

Think This:

"My work environment should never feel abusive, intimidating, or creepy." You owe it to yourself—and anyone else who may be experiencing similar treatment—to bravely speak up. When the offending party is your boss or other higher-level employee, it can certainly be nerve-racking to report the behavior. But try to find the courage to do so—you deserve to be treated with respect!

Say This:

"I feel really uncomfortable with what you just did and here's why."

"That was absolutely not okay."

"What did you just say?" (followed by stony silence)

"I'd prefer that you not touch me."

"Maybe you intended to be funny, but what you said offended me."

WHAT NEXT?

If you confront an inappropriate boss (or colleague) and it results in positive change, be proud of the change you initiated. Keep a close eye out to make sure the improvements stick and get back to delivering great work. If the person continues saying or doing things that cross the line, stay vigilant on documenting and reporting the issue. However, if your company is not addressing the bad behavior, you likely need to seek another job for your own well-being.

You Suspect Your Boss Is Trying to Sabotage You

Most bosses aim to be approachable and supportive, and are eager to help their team members grow. Unfortunately, some managers aren't like that—they may exert their power to keep you in a lower position, avoid recognizing your successes, assign you projects you're not ready for to see you fail, or just generally make your work life miserable. How should you respond if you find yourself in the crosshairs of a boss who seems to be out for you?

 Try these ideas to address this issue:

1 **Try stepping back to assess objectively.**
Are you being paranoid, or are your concerns valid? If it's hard for you to determine this on your own, ask a trusted peer.

2 **Stay calm.**
Even if you think you're onto something, it's best to stay levelheaded.

3 **Document everything.**
Save emails and messages, jot down notes about meetings, and so on.

4 **Take care of yourself.**
This terrible situation can take a toll on your physical and mental health. You'll be best able to respond if you eat well, get regular rest, and keep your head clear.

5 **Take action.**
Whether that's politely confronting your manager or going to HR, do what you can to get to the bottom of this.

DON'T CONVINCE YOURSELF THAT YOU'RE STUCK. Even if you're new on the job, really need the income, or had high hopes this would be a dream job, you don't need to show up for work every day facing a no-win situation. If your manager seems to be making it their mission to hold you down—and your efforts to improve the situation aren't working—you've got to make a change.

HERE'S HOW
These additional tips and scripts will help you as you confront and resolve the situation.

Think This:

"I bring many skills and talents to this job, so I will hold my head high as I deal with this situation." Here's something important to understand if your boss is sabotaging you: Their behavior is saying much more about *them* than it is about you. Your boss may see you as a threat (because you're awesome) and feel insecure and worried you'll outshine them. It's ridiculous, yes, but very possible.

Say This:

Say to your boss: "I've been getting the feeling that you don't want me to succeed with this client. Is there something about [action you've observed] that I'm misunderstanding?"

Say to a trusted ally: "Is it me, or have you noticed the same things?"

Say to HR: "I have documented these specific examples of my manager making work more difficult for me. Can we meet to review and determine next steps?"

WHAT NEXT?

If confronting the issue thoughtfully brought some resolution, proceed with cautious optimism. Consider building or strengthening your connections with other leaders within the company, and networking with people at companies of interest, just in case things go south again. If it's clear that you cannot grow or succeed under this manager, escalate the issue to an appropriate level (to your boss's boss, HR manager, or even an attorney) and/or begin your job search immediately.

You Need to Ask Your Boss for Special Arrangements

When taking on new jobs, most people don't consider what will happen if their circumstances change at some point: maybe you have a baby, need to care for an elderly parent, want to work from home, or experience burnout. But what if that "future" is right now and you need to change your work schedule or make accommodations to manage your current situation? How can you raise the issue?

 Try these ideas to address this issue:

1 Pick your timing strategically.
Think about the time and place that will best position you for a yes.

2 Spell out exactly what you need.
Asking your boss if you can work from 11 a.m. to 5 p.m. on Tuesdays and Fridays is much better than simply saying, "I just need fewer hours."

3 Highlight how your manager (or team) will benefit.
Sure, your special request may not come with any huge benefits to your employer, but if you envision that the arrangement will positively impact your performance, cut costs, or whatever, be sure to weave that into your pitch.

4 Suggest a trial period.
This may be particularly useful if they seem to be on the fence.

DON'T ASSUME THAT BECAUSE A COWORKER WAS APPROVED FOR SOME SPECIAL ARRANGEMENT, YOUR REQUEST WILL RECEIVE EQUAL CONSIDERATION. Your colleague may have different circumstances, or a different boss, or perhaps negotiated a different deal right from the start. (Since they were successful, though, you may want to check in with your teammate for pointers on how they gained approval.) At the very least, don't start your negotiations with, "Well, since so-and-so gets to work from home, I want to also."

HERE'S HOW

Beyond the basics, here's some additional food for thought that may be helpful.

Think This:

"This is a perfectly reasonable thing to ask for." Many employers have realized in recent years how beneficial flexible work arrangements (and honoring special requests) can be for everyone. Happy employees and those with solid work-life balance are going to outperform those who are feeling overwhelmed by their current situation. They also tend to stay in their jobs longer. (Hopefully, your boss knows this!)

Say This:

"We're getting close to the end of my maternity leave. Would you be available for a brief meeting to chat about my return plans?"

"My siblings and I will be sharing in the care of my eighty-year-old dad for a few months. Would you consider me working four ten-hour days per week through August?"

"I also anticipate I'll be able to call on two more clients every week by cutting out commute time."

WHAT NEXT? ⟶

If your manager agrees to a special arrangement for you, be sure to thank them, then work hard to show them the benefits of the new setup (to the company or them personally). If they are hesitant, again, float the idea of trying it out for thirty or sixty days and then evaluating together if it's working. And if their answer is no, decide if you can make current conditions work, or if you'll need to move on. (Remember, plenty of employers are offering flexibility with work arrangements today!)

You Need to Put In Your Notice

A graceful exit is the only way to go when you decide to quit your job. But when you're leaving a great boss and team (for an even more amazing opportunity), it's not always easy to do. You might feel guilty about leaving, uncertain of what you'll say, or anxious about having "the meeting" with your manager. Is it possible to get through this with confidence and composure?

 Try these ideas to address this issue:

1   **Get your affairs in order ahead of time.**
Are you due for an eye exam or unsure about how to roll over your 401(k)? Put these things on your to-do list right away. Likewise, use up any vacation days that you'll lose otherwise.

2   **Draft your resignation letter, then schedule the meeting.**
If possible, make it a face-to-face discussion. If you're working virtually, video conference will suffice.

3   **Be succinct and straightforward.**
State that you're resigning, propose an end date, and offer specific suggestions on how you can help smooth the transition (e.g., hand off projects, close out with clients, etc.).

4   **Be appreciative.**
Even if you truly despise the job (or boss) you're leaving, show gratitude for the opportunity and share something you've learned from the job or your manager.

5   **Breathe a sigh of relief.**
Mission accomplished.

YOU DON'T NEED TO APOLOGIZE, OVERTALK, OR PRO-VIDE EVERY LAST DETAIL ON WHAT YOU'RE DOING OR WHY. Even if you're feeling guilty (or even sad) about putting in your notice, remember: This is business. People come and people go, and things will continue on after you're gone (even if you're an amazing employee, which, of course you are). If your boss or coworkers are grumbly after learning the news, so be it. Hold your head high.

HERE'S HOW
Now that you're square on the basics, here are a few additional tips to help ensure a smooth exit.

Think This:	Say This:
"As the CEO of my own career, I need to do what's best for *my* business—the business of me." While it's certainly noble to be a loyal employee, here's something to keep in mind: If your employer was going through financial challenges or a restructure, they could have laid you off or eliminated your position—even if you're a beloved staff member. They'll do what's best for the business, always—so remind yourself that you're just doing the very same thing.	"Please accept my resignation from my position as ____. My last day of employment will be ____." "It's been a pleasure learning and growing under your direction. I've particularly appreciated your giving me the opportunity to ____." "To support the transition, I'll propose that I spend the remainder of my time focused on ____." "Thank you. I've really enjoyed working for you."

WHAT NEXT?

If your boss agrees to your proposed timeline and transition plan, concentrate on closing out exactly how you've offered to (and ask if there's anything else that would be helpful). If you're asked to leave immediately (which could happen), try not to take it personally. Plenty of companies have a policy about this, largely because they want to protect internal data and client information. Simply reiterate your gratitude for the opportunity and get excited about your next adventure!

Chapter 3

GETTING ALONG WITH YOUR COWORKERS

Working alongside people with diverse personalities, backgrounds, and areas of expertise can be energizing, rewarding, and a whole lot of fun. It can also be stressful and irritating from time to time. Someone is bound to get on your nerves every once in a while, and you're likely to do the same to someone else, even if you don't mean to. When those challenging situations with coworkers arise, this chapter will help you navigate whatever issues may crop up confidently and successfully.

This chapter will cover some of the most common issues that arise with coworkers, both the good (helping a new coworker find their way) and the bad (a workplace rife with cliques). So you'll know just what to say next time Shea from Accounting comes barging into your cube for what feels like the fiftieth time this week. You'll be more equipped to stand up to (or ignore) the office bully. And you'll be ready to ask that cool marketing director—who you *really* want to be friends with—out to lunch without it being completely awkward for either one of you.

Maintaining professional relationships with your coworkers while also thriving in your actual job can require strategy, patience, courage, and assertiveness. With luck, most of your workdays are happy and drama-free...but disagreements, annoying habits, and interruptions can happen occasionally in even the most positive work environments. Luckily, the skills you'll learn in this chapter will help you address those issues with confidence and grace. Let's get started.

Your Coworkers Are Very Cliquey

Anyone who went to high school probably remembers cliques—groups of people who used their perceived power to command superiority over others and exclude anyone they didn't like. As you entered the workforce, you probably assumed those days were over, right? Wrong. Office cliques are out there, and can be quite damaging to both the office environment and your personal well-being.

 Try these ideas to address this issue:

1 **Don't let them get to you.**
Cliquey people derive energy from knowing they're bothering you somehow. The more emotionless and work-focused you can be, the better.

2 **Be kind to and inclusive of everyone.**
This will present a clear sign to clique members that you value all types of people and, importantly, you're not recruitable.

3 **If you're being left out of after-work gatherings (and it bothers you), host your own.**
And when you do, include anyone who wants to join in—including the cliquey ones. (Yes, really.)

4 **Tell your manager.**
If a clique is undermining workplace morale, quietly report what's going on to your manager or an HR representative.

DON'T ASSUME EVERY TIGHT-KNIT GROUP OF FRIENDS IS A CLIQUE. To help tell the difference, ask yourself, "Is this group intentionally excluding me?" (the hallmark of a toxic clique) and "Is there anything I'm doing that may be signaling that I'm not interested in *them*?" (they could just be close friends who don't realize you'd like to hang out with them). If your coworkers move between groups with ease and don't seem to be going out of their way to gossip, bully, or alienate others, they're probably not a clique.

✓ HERE'S HOW

Now that you know how to identify and avoid cliques, here are additional tips that'll help you bypass, survive, or squash them.

Think This:

"Being an outsider might just be a great thing." By aligning with one group whose members likely look, think, and act an awful lot alike, you'll miss out on so much, like fresh perspectives, opportunities to learn new things, and the kind of personal growth that only comes from being around a wide range of people, to name a few.

Say This:

To avoid being recruited: "Unfortunately, I'm not available for happy hour tonight, but thanks for the invite."

To model inclusivity to a new employee: "Welcome to the team. Join me for lunch?"

If confrontation is merited: "It feels like this group is intentionally leaving people out. Can we try to be more welcoming?"

If you're the boss: "I've noticed that the vibe around here isn't as friendly as it could be. We're going to hold a whole-division retreat to get to know everyone better."

WHAT NEXT? ⟶

If you get to a place of resolution, acceptance, or peace with the office clique, keep an eye out for others who may be suffering from their awful ways. Support them and, if they're open to it, offer your thoughts on how you were able to deal with the situation. If you've made constructive efforts to deal with the clique, but the group continues to make it difficult or impossible for you to thrive, get help. Ask a mentor, your boss, a counselor, or HR for guidance. Or, in the worst case, start looking for a new job.

Your Coworkers Keep Undermining Your Decisions or Expertise

Whether taking credit for your work, intentionally causing you to miss deadlines, or finding endless ways to cut you down, underminers are a dangerous breed. Left unchecked, they can create all kinds of distress and could even jeopardize your job. How should you respond to someone who keeps undercutting you at work?

 Try these ideas to address this issue:

1. **Ask yourself, "Is this run-of-the-mill competitiveness or actual undermining?"**
   If it's a hypercompetitive colleague who approaches life in full conquer mode, remember that being competitive doesn't equal sabotage. Underminers deliberately try to impede your success.

2. **Track the infractions.**
   Are they purposely withholding information, spreading rumors, or excluding you from important meetings? Take detailed notes in case you need to seek help from management or HR.

3. **Ask for clarification.**
   For example, if it seems they've intentionally failed to disclose a deadline, you can say, "So-and-so, why didn't you tell me that our boss needed this by Wednesday?"

4. **Stop sharing nonvital information with them.**

DON'T STICK YOUR HEAD IN THE SAND AND HOPE THINGS GO AWAY. If your coworker's actions have potential to damage your professional reputation or even jeopardize your job, you can't ignore them. Keep in mind: You're only seeing this person's overt behavior. You never know what they're up to behind the scenes. If they're dedicated to bringing you down, they could also be manipulating others, and things could end very badly for you.

✔ HERE'S HOW

Here are a few additional things to consider and say when dealing with coworkers who seem to be sabotaging you.

Think This:	Say This:
"This probably isn't about me." When someone undermines you, their behavior usually relates more to them (and their insecurities) than it does to you. Chances are they're so insecure about their own abilities (or envious of you) that they see pulling you down as their only way to look good in front of the boss, clients, or colleagues. If you can look at the situation through this lens—and try to either muster a bit of empathy or detach emotionally—you'll be much better equipped to manage the situation than if you're visibly enraged or demoralized.	"I noticed you deleted the data I'd need to finish the project. Why'd you do that?" "Why did you make a joke about my college degree in the meeting?" "Next time you have an issue with my work, I'd appreciate your talking to me privately instead of embarrassing me in front of a group." "Did you intend to make me look bad in front of our customers today?"

WHAT NEXT? ⟶

With luck, by calling out or questioning your teammate's cheap shots, you'll make them realize the error of their ways and knock it off—or at least know that you're not one to be messed with. If, however, they continue with their subversive ways, take all that evidence you've gathered to management and ask them to step in. Because no employee needs (or deserves) work to feel like stepping onto a battlefield.

You Overhear a Private (and Not Complimentary) Conversation about You

You're moseying down the hall at work and, as you approach the conference room, you hear the familiar voices of your teammates. Before they realize you're within earshot, you realize what those voices are saying. They're talking about you, and it's not at all complimentary. You're hurt, you're mad, and you've got mere seconds to figure out what to do. What's your next move?

 Try these ideas to address this issue:

1 **Walk in with a smile on your face and say hello.**
That will silence the room very quickly.

2 **Use humor.**
Slide in quietly and add to the conversation to let them know you overheard. Say you heard, "She never stops talking about her dumb dog." Try chiming in with, "And I hear she's a terrible cook."

3 **If it's mean or incorrect, call it out.**
Complaining that you always leave dishes in the breakroom sink is a lot different than calling you names or saying something truly off-base. If it's the latter, speak up.

4 **Ignore it entirely.**
If you know what they're saying is untrue and it's not even worth your time, ignore it and walk away unnoticed.

DON'T RETALIATE. When someone says something unthoughtful, untrue, or just plain mean behind your back, it definitely stings— and your immediate thought might be to make that person feel the burn right back. But seeking revenge is a bad idea, for a lot of reasons. First, it may not make you feel better. In fact, being retaliatory could make you feel worse, especially since you're probably a kind, fair, and respectful human being. Further, if you do or say something nasty and get caught, it may actually be *you* who ends up in hot water.

✓ HERE'S HOW

Consider these tips and talking points as you figure out how you'll tackle the issue.

Think This:

"Maybe this person dislikes confrontation." People who talk behind your back may lack the courage, assertiveness, or character that it takes to bring issues they have with you to your attention directly. This certainly doesn't excuse their behavior, but try to extract a lesson from this experience. The next time *you're* tempted to complain about someone behind *their* back—try instead having a constructive (and kind) face-to-face conversation.

Say This:

"Is there something we need to discuss?"

"You know that I'm standing right here, right?"

"Yikes, this is awkward. Shall I come back in a few minutes?"

"Hmmm…I've not heard that one about me before. Usually people focus more on my witty personality and dashing good looks."

"If you're panicking a little bit because I just overheard that, don't even sweat it."

WHAT NEXT? ➝

If you've said your piece and everyone seems apologetic or appropriately sheepish, get back to business. We all vent sometimes, even when we really should address the matter directly (or just zip it). If, however, this seems to be a chronic issue, or it's eroding your well-being, weigh the pros and cons of sticking around. A professional environment should, in fact, be professional. If yours consistently isn't, set your sights on finding one that is.

You Are Considering Recommending a Friend for an Open Position with Your Company

Companies tend to really value referred candidates when they're looking to fill open roles. And that's understandable—current employees understand the business and typically have a pulse on who would be a great fit, culture-wise. And if you have a friend who needs a job, it can be a real win-win situation. But have you considered the pros and cons first?

 Try these ideas to address this issue:

1 **Ask yourself, "Is my friend likely to thrive in this job?"**
Try to answer the question in an honest and objective manner. You surely don't want to refer someone who's a poor match for the position or your company overall, even if your friend really needs a job right now.

2 **Investigate your company's referral program.**
More specifically, see if your firm offers employees financial incentive for recommending qualified candidates. If they do, be sure to make the introduction in a way that aligns with the program's requirements.

3 **Introduce your friend thoughtfully.**
You probably have a hunch which traits your boss will value the most. Lead with that.

4 **Be their cheerleader, but don't sugarcoat.**
When you agree to refer someone, represent them well; at the same time, don't stretch the truth.

DON'T RECOMMEND SOMEONE IF YOUR GUT SAYS THAT REFERRAL MAY COME BACK TO HAUNT YOU (EVEN IF YOUR BUDDY'S PRESSURING YOU). Instead, weigh the needs of your organization against your assessment of your friend's qualifications and fit. If you suspect that their skills and experience just won't set them up for success, think twice before making the introduction. Remember, your reputation is on the line, and your friend deserves to be happy and successful too.

HERE'S HOW Here are a few more things to think about and say as you proceed with recommending your friend.

Think This:

"I should be thoughtful about recommendations, but not so afraid that I avoid them entirely." Think of the potentially powerful win-win-win scenario: Your buddy wins by landing a new job. They'll also likely settle in pretty quickly with you in the mix. The company wins by finding a qualified candidate—likely faster and at a lower cost than if they'd needed to outsource the effort. And you win by having a direct say in the evolution and growth of the organization.

Say This:

"It seems you're looking for someone with both design skills and writing experience, correct? I have someone great in mind."

"What's the best way for me to introduce my contact to you?"

"Beyond their obvious experience, here's what I think makes them a great fit."

"Here's a link to their LinkedIn profile for a quick peek."

WHAT NEXT?

Should your friend land an interview, help them put their best foot forward as they move through the hiring process. (And, of course, be front and center as they settle into the job.) If your employer decides not to hire your referred candidate, don't cop an attitude. Instead, ask for feedback on why they've made this decision. It may help you ease the sting for your friend and, also, prompt ideas for another potential fit.

You and Your Coworker Just Don't Get Along

In a perfect world, we would appreciate all of our colleagues. We'd value one another's differences and take advantage of the opportunity to learn from each other. We live in the real world, however, and sometimes you just don't like one of your coworkers. Maybe they're crass or annoying or just incredibly difficult to get along with. When you find yourself on the same team with someone you don't mesh with, what can you do about it?

 Try these ideas to address this issue:

1 **Remember that you won't likely hit it off with *everyone* you meet.**
Keep your expectations realistic.

2 **Assess *your* potential contributions.**
While you can probably whip up a list of every way your colleague drives you nuts, have you also considered the ways in which your behavior may be bothering that person? See if there's anything you can do to adjust your behavior accordingly.

3 **Create healthy boundaries.**
If you're just oil and water with a coworker, try identifying and implementing solutions that minimize your exposure to one another (and, at the same time, make life better for everyone in the mix).

4 **Don't let them get to you.**
No matter how abrasive your coworker is, strive to remain levelheaded.

5 **Extend an olive branch.**
Even if you feel strongly that you're not the violating party, you may benefit greatly by being the adult in the room and extending an invitation to find common ground.

DON'T LOSE YOUR TEMPER. Even if you and a coworker legitimately despise one another—and they've just said or done something that's irrefutably out of line—you simply cannot blow a fuse on them in the middle of the office. Likewise, think twice before airing your grievances on social media. Both responses could land you in hot water with the boss (or HR), damage your reputation among colleagues, or even get you fired. Cool down before speaking up.

HERE'S HOW

Once you've got the essentials down, try these additional tips and talking points as you work to resolve the tension between you and your colleague.

Think This:

"Could this be about something non-work-related?" Try to have compassion and realize that we're all dealing with issues that people at work may not know about. While all adults need to be accountable for their behavior in the workplace, this person may be stressed, anxious, or frustrated about something you are not aware of. If you realize that your peer's behavior may be due to external factors, perhaps you can cut them a bit of slack.

Say This:

"We seem to have gotten off on the wrong foot. Can I buy you a coffee?"

"Let's just divide up the work and focus on getting this project done. Sound good?"

"I know it bothers you when I interrupt you. I'll try not to do that anymore, okay?"

"You may not realize it, but what you said was quite hurtful."

WHAT NEXT?

If you're successful in reducing the contentiousness between you and your teammate, great. Can you take it one step further? Sometimes, once you break down the barriers that caused the tension in the first place, you set the groundwork for a new and healthier way of interacting. If you've given it your best shot yet realize that you'll probably never see eye to eye, it's probably best to keep interaction to a minimum. Be polite and respectful...from a distance.

You're Unhappy with the Company Culture

When you're applying for a job, it is sometimes difficult to gauge company culture during a few short interviews. Plus, everyone's on their best behavior when they're recruiting, so you might not see what day-to-day life is really like in that workplace. Given this, it's not unheard of to find yourself in a great job at a company whose culture just doesn't suit you. What then?

 Try these ideas to address this issue:

1 **Address the situation sooner rather than later.**
Don't let your unhappiness fester.

2 **Ask yourself what, specifically, isn't working.**
Is there a disconnect between management and staff? Are people always arguing? Are new ideas routinely disregarded? Do employees seem unhappy?

3 **See if anything can be done.**
Determine if you can resolve any of those situations, find a workaround, or reframe your mindset to make things satisfactory.

4 **If the place is truly infected, find a new job, then resign, promptly.**
Shifting company culture is challenging even in decent work environments and requires commitment from the top. If that's clearly absent, you are probably not going to be able to fix it by yourself.

DON'T MAKE ANY KNEE-JERK DECISIONS TO QUIT IF YOU'RE JUST SETTLING INTO A NEW JOB. You might need time to get acclimated and find your people. Many companies (especially larger ones) have subgroups—clubs, sports leagues, social groups, etc. See if you can find one you like. Of course, if you observe notable drama or fighting or a glaring misalignment of values, that's a different situation, and you shouldn't wait months to get yourself out of that environment.

HERE'S HOW
Now that you're clear on the dos and don'ts, here are a few more things to think about and say as you work through the situation.

Think This:	Say This:
"How can I avoid another similar situation in the future?" What could you pay closer attention to through the interview process next time? What questions can you ask that will help you figure out what's going on inside the organization? What will serve as immediate red flags? Try thinking about what may, at first, feel like a career misstep as a valuable learning experience instead.	"What are the company values?" "How would you describe the work environment?" "Can you describe the ideal person for this role?" "What does work-life balance look like?" "Would you describe the company as collaborative or competitive?" "What makes you proud to work here?" "How are accomplishments recognized?" "How is conflict handled?"

WHAT NEXT? ⟶

If you've gotten over the early discomfort of not fitting in and discovered that there really is much to appreciate about your company's culture, fantastic. If, however, you've proactively attempted to find your "spot," yet are still feeling strong misalignment, you may want to begin a job search. Unless you're in a position of power, you won't likely be successful in influencing major changes to the overall culture.

Your Coworker Is Nosy or Overly Inquisitive

Unless you work alone or for a very small company, you're bound to have that one coworker who just loves to dive into everyone's business. It may seem reasonably funny and harmless, unless you're the one who always seems to be on the receiving end of the office Nosy Nellie's prying ways. Is it possible to nip the behavior in the bud while keeping things (at least somewhat) friendly?

 Try these ideas to address this issue:

1   **Decide how to handle it.**
    Generally speaking, you have three choices when it comes to an overly inquisitive teammate: avoid, deflect, or confront. Pick one, then try the following suggestions based on your choice.

2   **Avoid:**
    The more unavailable you can look when the office busybody comes by, the better. Start madly clattering on your keyboard, pretend to take an urgent call, or (if permitted) wear headphones as you work.

3   **Deflect:**
    Try redirecting the topic back to work ("Why am I not married yet? Not sure. Did you have a work question?") or responding with a humorous nonanswer ("Where do I live? In another state. Haven't you seen my helicopter out in the parking lot?"), then walk away.

4   **Confront:**
    If the behavior feels truly invasive or inappropriate, you should talk about it directly. Take a private moment and let your coworker know that you prefer to keep your personal life personal, so please don't ask you about nonwork matters again.

DON'T FEEL LIKE YOU OWE YOUR NOSY COLLEAGUE AN ANSWER. Sure, it can be super tricky to get away from a conversation you don't want to participate in without alienating the other person, but you get to decide how much personal information you're going to share at work. If you're confrontation averse, try to work on establishing healthy boundaries and shutting down intrusive conversations. (If you're afraid of seeming rude, remember that *they* should feel rude for trying to invade your bubble!)

HERE'S HOW

Now that you know how to address or avert a meddlesome colleague (and how not to), use these tips to ensure a successful outcome.

Think This:

"I should assume good intentions." Certainly, some coworkers seem to derive energy and a sense of worth by being the one who always gets the scoop. But others may come across as nosy or intrusive but could just be (clumsily) trying to get to know you better. They may have a hard time forging friendships or struggle socially in general. If you suspect this may be the case, show some grace.

Say This:

"I do have a boyfriend, yes. Say, how's everything coming with the market analysis?"

"Interesting question. I'm so sorry, but I need to focus on an urgent issue right now. Chat later?"

"Hahahaha! For a second, I thought you were seriously asking me to answer that question at work. You're funny!"

"I don't discuss that at work, sorry."

WHAT NEXT?

If you realize that your teammate means well—and is actually *nice* under that annoying shell—fabulous. Perhaps you can gently encourage them to adopt new ways in getting to know others. If it appears to be a lost cause—that the intrusive behavior is a cornerstone to who they are—keep your "avoid, deflect, confront" tools at the ready so you can use them whenever needed. And remember, *you* decide what to share.

Your Coworker Doesn't Complete Their Work On Schedule

When your team is firing on all cylinders, it's a magical thing. You produce great work together and, likely, have fun in the process. But when you've got a slacker in the mix, it can become not so fun pretty quickly, especially if they create a bottleneck that prevents you from getting *your* work done. What should you do if you find yourself working alongside someone who can't seem to get their act together?

 Try these ideas to address this issue:

1 **Ask yourself if it's truly impacting you, or just bugging you.**
If the latter, it's probably best to not say anything at all. Surely, the boss will catch on to their lazy ways sooner or later.

2 **Speak up, kindly.**
If your coworker's ways are putting your performance at risk, find a gentle way to point out the ripple effect going on.

3 **If you have the bandwidth, offer to support them, but don't do all of their work for them.**
Likewise, don't cover for them. That won't help you or the team long term.

4 **As a last resort, go to your manager.**
Present the facts and ask for input on how to best handle the situation. You don't want to look like the office tattletale, so present it as an issue that's affecting the company's potential.

DON'T BERATE YOUR COWORKER PUBLICLY OR BAD-MOUTH THEM TO OTHER TEAM MEMBERS, EVEN IF YOU'RE BEYOND FRUSTRATED. That's not going to resolve anything and may, in fact, make the situation worse. Unless you're this person's manager, it's really not your place to give them that type of feedback anyway.

HERE'S HOW

Now that you've got the basics down, here are a few extra tips and talking points to try as you work to resolve the situation.

Think This:

"I will approach this person with some empathy." There are a lot of reasons why someone might fall behind in their work. Try to find compassion and assume good intentions—they may want to finish things on time, but for some reason cannot. Maybe they need more training. Maybe there's something going on behind the scenes in that person's personal life. Adopting a kindhearted mindset will likely help you and the person move forward in the most productive way possible.

Say This:

"I noticed that you missed the past couple of deadlines. Can I help you get caught up on anything?"

"We seem to be hitting a slow-down when it comes to your deliverables lately. Is something wrong?"

"When you don't complete your work on time, I can't get mine done on time. What can we do to resolve this?"

WHAT NEXT?

If, after tactfully confronting your teammate, you see improvements, consider it a job well done, for both you and the company. Sometimes, people just need a little nudge in the right direction. If the snail-like pace seems to be entrenched, however—and particularly if it's negatively impacting your performance—don't let it fester. Point your colleague to resources that may help them get on track and/or alert your manager. Don't allow their lack of productivity to get *you* into trouble.

You Are Thinking about Dating a Coworker

Given the percentage of waking hours most of us spend at work, office romance should come as no surprise. You don't just share time and space with one another; you also probably have some common interests, goals, and plenty of opportunity to see one another. But dating a coworker comes with certain risks. So, what should you do if you're thinking about going down that road?

 Try these ideas to address this issue:

1 **Find out if your employer has a policy related to dating among coworkers.**
   Plenty do, largely to mitigate risk of a sexual harassment claim arising.

2 **Think about what you'll do if your relationship goes sideways.**
   It's all fine and well if you stay together, but if you don't, things could be very awkward at work. Consider how you'll proceed if the romance sours.

3 **Commit to taking things slow.**
   Even in the best of circumstances, an office romance is going to be complicated. You'll be wise to pace yourselves and make sure it's worth the extra effort.

4 **Establish ground rules in advance.**
   Do you tell no one? Just your boss? Everyone? Do you eat lunch together? Date other coworkers if you break up? You get the drift.

DON'T DATE YOUR BOSS OR A DIRECT REPORT. Aside from the obvious risks this presents—distraction during the workday, gossip or resentment among coworkers, potential sharing of confidential information, and so forth—you may put yourself at risk of being fired (especially if you're the boss, since you're in the position of power). If you have your heart set on dating your manager or a subordinate, this may be the right time for one of you to leave the firm.

HERE'S HOW

Use these tips and questions as you evaluate the office romance decision to ensure things unfold as smoothly as possible.

Think This:	**Say This:**
"If we move forward, we'll need to act appropriately in the office." Keep your coworkers in mind if your relationship moves forward. Even if you're *certain* you've landed the most incredible mate on the planet, keep your PDA out of the office. No quick smooches in the breakroom, no lingering hugs in the parking lot. The last thing you want to do is jeopardize your professional reputations by making your coworkers feel uncomfortable.	"Are you married?" "What will we do if this becomes serious?" "What will we do if we break up?" "Which specific people are we going to tell?" "What will we say if anyone we haven't told asks us if we're dating?" "How will we respond if people gossip?" "Do you think it'll be worth it?"

WHAT NEXT?

If you decide to move forward with an office romance, make sure the relationship doesn't interfere with your work performance. Keep in mind that your employer didn't hire you so that you could find your soul mate. When you're in one another's company *outside* of the office, though, enjoy your downtime! You don't have to talk about work all the time. If you decide not to move forward, consider that maybe your timing was off and things will unfold between you when one of you no longer works at the company.

Your Coworker Keeps Taking Your Lunch Out of the Communal Fridge

It sounds cliché, but it's real: the lunch thief, who consistently and unapologetically raids the breakroom fridge, swiping anything that looks remotely tasty—regardless of whose it is or how many "not your food" sticky notes are plastered on the container. When you're the one whose food is being stolen, it's not just irritating—it feels like a violation. What's the best way to stop a sandwich-scrounging coworker?

 Try these ideas to address this issue:

1 **Invest in a well-insulated lunch bag or personal fridge and keep your food right in your cubicle or office.**
Voilà! Fresh food at your fingertips whenever the mood strikes.

2 **Go nuts with a Sharpie.**
Sticky notes can be easily removed. Make it hard for the pilferer to go unnoticed by writing all over your stuff in permanent marker.

3 **Bring your food in an unusual (and very noticeable) container.**
Nondescript takeout containers are a lot easier to swipe than something in, say, a neon tote or expensive-looking bento box.

4 **Label your delicious leftovers as something no one will touch.**
(Breast milk, anyone?)

DON'T DO ANYTHING YOU'LL REGRET. Google this topic, and you'll find some downright wicked recommendations, like loading your hoagie with hot sauce (or worse), leaving long-expired leftovers for unsuspecting scavengers, or hooking up a webcam (which may be against company policy) to catch them in the act. As angry as you may be, refrain from making any retaliatory response.

HERE'S HOW   Now that you've calmed down, here are things to think and say as you work to resolve the incredibly maddening situation.

Think This:

"Forgive and forget!" If you figure out who the culprit is, try hard to drum up at least a bit of compassion for your lunch looter. Chances are, they're not a horrible person but a hungry one who never stopped to think about how their actions were inconsiderate and, in fact, theft. If the behavior stops, try to leave the whole incident behind you.

Say This:

"You guys! Someone took my sandwich and I just realized the meat was expired. Don't anyone eat that!"

"I'm sure you didn't realize that was my soda, but I see my name is on the bottom of it. Do you mind checking next time?"

"Are you hungry? If so, let me buy you lunch tomorrow."

WHAT NEXT?

If your efforts are successful, congratulations. Great news—your work in putting an end to this behavior may just help others in the process. If, however, the pillaging continues, you should alert your manager. This is, after all, theft, and no one should expect burglary when at the office.

Your Coworker Never Stops Complaining

Some people just seem to have one negative thing to say after another. Rather than bringing energy and positivity into the environment, they seem to drag everyone around them down with their endless complaints, quibbles, and criticisms about everything from the weather to the ways of the world. When you work with a constant complainer, it can be more than annoying: According to a University of Wisconsin School of Medicine study, it can impact your productivity and even be detrimental to your health.

 Try these ideas to address this issue:

1. **Acknowledge their concerns, to a point.**
   Sometimes, complainers are just looking to feel heard. A simple "I can imagine that was frustrating" might go a long way.

2. **Ask if they want your advice.**
   Are they venting or looking for a way to reframe or address the situation?

3. **If they do want advice, challenge them to come up with solutions.**
   Do it in a nice way, of course, but try asking for their thoughts around how to solve whatever they're grumping about.

4. **Call them out...politely.**
   Mention that you're noticing a lot of negativity from them lately and wondering if everything's okay.

5. **Change the subject.**
   That horrible waiter they had last night sounds awful but, hey, let's dive into this meeting agenda.

DON'T MINDLESSLY VALIDATE WHATEVER THING THAT THE OFFICE CRANK IS COMPLAINING ABOUT JUST TO GET THROUGH THE CONVERSATION. While that tactic sounds completely harmless, you may be inadvertently agreeing to be their go-to person for this and all future grievances. Assuming that's not what you want, avoid this brush-off strategy. You're not responsible for being the recipient of all of this person's negative energy, so don't feel like you need to stand there nodding.

✔ HERE'S HOW

As you master the dos and don'ts, consider these additional tips for figuring out how to manage your complaining coworker.

Think This:

"Why might this person be complaining so much?" Most often, it's because expectations were one thing, and reality was another. For instance, maybe you expected gorgeous weather on your wedding day and got rain. The complainer likely is dwelling on these types of situations. You might think about whether you ever dabble in this behavior, and how you can change your mindset.

Say This:

"Oh, man. You seem to run into a lot of traffic issues. Have you considered changing your route?"

"That does sound like a drag. Have you thought about how you might resolve the issue?"

"I know you might just be looking to blow off steam, but I'm happy to share my thoughts if you'd like any advice."

WHAT NEXT?

If you're able to get your point across and reduce the number of complaints you're subjected to, consider it a win. If it's apparent that whining is simply in their DNA, you may need to get a bit more direct and tell them you don't want to hear all the negative thoughts. You can't change people who don't wish to change, but you can let them know that you're not willing to be their sounding board.

You Want to Help a New Coworker Settle In

You've been there before: those awkward first days and weeks in a brand-new job. You surely recall how nerve-racking setting up shop in an unfamiliar environment—with unfamiliar people, processes, and norms—can be. You also realize that your just-hired colleague is likely feeling much the same right about now, and you want to help reduce their stress as they settle in. But you don't want to seem overbearing or like a know-it-all either. How should you proceed?

 Try these ideas to address this issue:

1 **Ask their manager what you can do.**
Not that you need permission to welcome a colleague, but their supervisor likely has onboarding plans too. Try synching your efforts.

2 **Show them around.**
When you're new, you've got a million things to figure out—processes, systems, job responsibilities, you name it. Take "find the conference room" off their list of worries by giving them a quick tour.

3 **Take them to coffee or lunch.**
If you're pressed for time or money, at least sit with them in the cafeteria.

4 **Answer the potentially embarrassing questions they may have...before they need to ask.**
(e.g., "Here's the bathroom" or "Push this button if the printer starts beeping loudly").

5 **If they're new to the area, share a list of local "bests"—best sandwiches, best coffee, best pizza slices, best diner.**
People always appreciate knowing the top places nearby.

DON'T MAKE YOUR COWORKER FEEL UNCOMFORTABLE OR ENCROACHED UPON BY YOUR WELCOMING WAYS. Recognize that there's a fine line between "you're so considerate" and "yikes, back off!" Be available, for sure. They'll probably want some time to focus and figure things out on their own and get their workspace organized. They may be shy or introverted. Follow the cues of your colleague in determining how and when you'll help them get acclimated.

✔ HERE'S HOW

As you head over to greet your new teammate, here are a few more things to think about and say.

Think This:

"This new coworker has a *lot* going on right now." While everyone's experience is unique, the swirl of emotions that accompanies those first days and weeks in a new role is universal. It's an exciting time for many, but realize your new coworker could be missing their former job, frustrated over the learning curve, self-conscious about their outfit, or scared they'll make a goof. No matter how you decide to help your teammate find their footing, be kind and patient.

Say This:

"Welcome! We're excited to have you here."

"Do you already have plans for lunch? If not, want to join us?"

"Can I show you around the place?"

"Are there any supplies that you need but don't yet have?"

"Someone brought in amazing doughnuts this morning. Can I get you one?"

"Our expense reporting process is a beast. Want me to show you?"

WHAT NEXT? ⟶

If your teammate seems to be settling in smoothly after a few days on the job, great! It's always nice to feel like you've had a hand in the success of others. Remind them that you're available for questions, then give them space to find their groove. If you suspect that they're still struggling to learn the ropes after a couple of weeks, check in. See how things are going and let them know that you're happy to assist.

Your Coworkers Keep Interrupting You When You Need to Focus

In our modern world, creating space for deep thinking can be very difficult. We live in an era of open floor plans, instant gratification, and wild celebration over one's ability to multitask. Given this, it should come as no surprise when you find yourself with coworkers who don't think twice about interrupting you whenever the moment strikes them. Assuming that *doesn't* work for you, what then?

 Try these ideas to address this issue:

1 **Be honest.**
It's weird how nervous people get about shutting down an interrupter when, in fact, they're the ones getting bothered. Speak up, with kindness.

2 **Make it easier for people to see that you're tied up.**
If you're virtual, set your profile as unavailable or create a detailed out-of-office message. If you're in a physical office, create an easy visual system so people can see when you're not to be disturbed.

3 **Clarify when you *are* available.**
If you check email or voicemail every morning at 9 a.m. and then again at 4 p.m. or keep thirty minutes open every afternoon for face time with colleagues, make sure people know this.

4 **Relocate.**
There's no shame in hiding out in an empty conference room if that's the only way you can concentrate on the task at hand.

DON'T JUMP RIGHT TO THE CONCLUSION THAT THEY'RE BEING INCONSIDERATE JERKS WHEN PEOPLE INTERRUPT YOU. They may have come from a work environment that encouraged impromptu collaboration among coworkers. They may not realize you're on an important deadline. You never know. In any case, don't let your emotions get the best of you. Take a few moments to calm down before confronting them with your feelings and proposed solutions.

HERE'S HOW
Let's take a look at a few more ideas and phrases you can use in addressing office interlopers.

Think This:

"Interruptions might not *always* be a bad thing." On one hand, study after study confirms that workplace interruptions are indeed a problematic disruption. When employees don't have ample time to think critically, assess problems, or birth new ideas, it's not just productivity that suffers; it's also company performance. But, on the other hand, emerging research reported by *ScienceDaily* suggests that interruptions may also have an upside in that they can help employees feel a stronger sense of belonging.

Say This:

"I'd love to hear all about this later, but I'm afraid I need to stay focused on this right now."

"I'm sure your engagement pictures are gorgeous. May I stop by your cube at 4 p.m. to look at them?"

"If my door is open, please just come right in. If it's closed, that means I need time to concentrate, but feel free to leave a note."

WHAT NEXT?

Even if you make great progress in curbing your office interruptions, try to be understanding about the periodic slipups. Unfortunately, most of us are fully immersed in this instant gratification culture; we may not even realize we are creating a problem. Now, if a coworker is simply refusing to honor your request, then it's probably time to establish stronger boundaries or ask your manager to assist. You surely have big goals—they deserve your full focus.

Your Coworker Has an Annoying (or Gross) Habit

We are all guilty of annoying our coworkers, at least some of the time. But some employees have a special knack for taking "annoying" to extreme, offensive, or truly unbearable levels. They'll unapologetically burp (or worse) in meetings, sing along with the tunes they're piping through their earphones, heat up strong-smelling leftovers for lunch, or clip their toenails anytime—and anywhere—the mood strikes. How should you respond if your coworker doesn't share the same definition of "office appropriate"?

 Try these ideas to address this issue:

1   **Be direct.**
    Now, this doesn't mean "be rude and direct," but if your teammate is doing something out of line, wait until you're calm and ask them if they could do [gross thing] outside of the common workspace.

2   **Shield yourself.**
    Earplugs or a plug-in air freshener might help you get by quite nicely.

3   **Ask your manager to help.**
    If it's truly disruptive stuff that you're dealing with—and you either don't feel comfortable sharing your feelings or are being ignored—there's no shame in asking your boss to step in.

DON'T RESORT TO PASSIVE AGGRESSIVE TACTICS AS YOU TRY TO MAKE A POINT. No one in the office wants to be subjected to your notes about hygiene on the bathroom mirrors or louder singing at your desk. Be the mature adult you are and proceed accordingly.

HERE'S HOW

In addition to these core tips, here are a few more things to think and say if you're challenged by a coworker's annoying tendencies:

Think This:

"Am I being unreasonable or culturally obtuse about what constitutes 'annoying' or 'gross'?" In a diverse workplace, you'll be alongside people with varying cultural norms, standards, and traditions. Consider this before you say something ignorant or hurtful.

Say This:

"I need you to know how unsettling it is to me when you burp so loudly while I'm on client calls."

"Could you give me a heads-up when you plan to reheat seafood? It's not my favorite smell, so I'll go for a little walk while you eat lunch at your desk."

"I'm putting earplugs in so I can concentrate. Give me a wave if you need me for anything, OK?"

WHAT NEXT?

If you've kindly requested that your colleague knock off the irritating behavior—and they've obliged—be sure to express your appreciation. Realize that it may actually be hard for them to, say, not crack their knuckles all day long or hum along to their favorite songs. If you've asked, but the behavior continues (despite a manager's involvement)—or your teammate becomes combative—it's time to schedule a chat with HR.

You Want to Be Friends with Your Coworkers Outside of the Workplace

Many kids are able to just stroll up to one another, start building a sandcastle together, and quickly wind up fast friends. As adults, however, it seems so much harder to cultivate friendships. We're out of practice. We're less carefree. We're *tired*. Nevertheless, most of us still want great friends, and we spend a lot of time at the office. What's the grown-up way to find sandcastle-building mates in the workplace?

 Try these ideas to address this issue:

1 Attend organized after-work events.
You'll have the opportunity to see other people out of the office setting and get to know them in a more casual manner.

2 Ask if they'd like to grab lunch.
Everybody takes at least a few minutes to eat during the workday, right?

3 Take a chance.
Is there someone you think is particularly cool and friendly—and seems to appreciate you as well? Be up front. Tell them you'd love to hang out. They probably won't know otherwise.

4 Take it slow.
The best relationships build up over time, adult friendships included.

DON'T GET OVERBEARING ABOUT IT IF YOUR COWORKER DOESN'T SEEM RECEPTIVE TO YOUR ATTEMPTS TO FORGE A CONNECTION. We all know *that* person—the one who latches onto people way too quickly and tries to become insta-besties with every new face in the office. Sure, work friendships are important to your well-being. But just because *you* want to become buds with a particular coworker doesn't mean the feeling will be reciprocated. If signs indicate that your timing is off, or that the other person just isn't looking to connect, let it be for now.

HERE'S HOW Now that you know what to do and what to stay away from, use these tips as you work to fire up an office friendship.

Think This:

"The effort it takes to make friends is worth it." There are a million reasons why making friends feels so hard when we're adults—self-consciousness, fear of rejection, lack of time, introversion, to name a few. But, study after study has shown that having good friends can reduce stress and anxiety, increase happiness, decrease loneliness, mitigate the risk of unhealthy habits, and help you rebound from health issues more quickly. You have more to gain than lose by recruiting friends from work!

Say This:

"You like hot wings? I was thinking about getting some after work this week. Join me?"

"I'm heading to happy hour. Want to come?"

"I play on a coed volleyball team on Wednesdays and we need a few more players. Anyone like volleyball?"

"Do you want to go hiking or mountain biking some weekend?"

WHAT NEXT?

If you're successful in building friendships with your coworkers, your workdays will likely become more fulfilling and your life richer overall. If you're finding the process challenging, or even experiencing rejection, try not to take it too personally. Sometimes finding your people takes time, especially when your coworkers have piles of demands or just aren't there to socialize. Give yourself the time and grace you need to go about this process with intention and care. You'll be glad you did!

You're Dealing with an Office Bully

When people talk about bullying, it's often in relation to the challenges that children face. But unfortunately, those bullies grow up, and, if their toxic behavior goes unchecked, they bring their bullying ways right into the workplace. Many of us have worked with an office bully. In fact, according to the Workplace Bullying Institute, 30 percent of working professionals have experienced some form of bullying at work, and 19 percent have witnessed it. If you're among the unlucky ones dealing with it right now, what should you do?

 Try these ideas to address this issue:

1 **Speak up.**
Be direct and be clear. Let your bully know their abuse is unacceptable and that you expect them to stop, immediately.

2 **Document everything.**
You'll need evidence if you decide to take the matter to your manager or HR. If the bullying is being done via email, you've already got a paper trail. If it's verbal, keep clear notes on the specifics of every encounter.

3 **Do some research.**
While there is no federal law that specifically bans workplace bullying (yet), your company may very well have an anti-bullying policy. Likewise, depending on the specifics of the situation, you may be protected by laws related to workplace harassment.

4 **Focus on self-care.**
When work becomes a battleground, it can take a toll on your physical and mental health. Be sure to prioritize your well-being—even if that ultimately means finding another job.

DON'T IGNORE THE SITUATION OR TRY TO EXPLAIN AWAY THEIR BAD BEHAVIOR. Though it may seem like you're taking the high road, staying silent likely won't make bullying magically disappear. You do not deserve this treatment, and standing up for yourself may be difficult in the short term, but it will likely be worthwhile in the long run.

HERE'S HOW
Use these additional ideas and sample scripts as you deal with the office bully.

Think This:

"I need to take care of myself." When you're on the receiving end of a bully, it can be extremely stressful and erode your self-confidence. And while you don't have control over the actions of an abusive colleague, you do have considerable say in your own. Think about using the situation as an opportunity to double down on your own self-care, so that you're in a better frame of mind to confront them directly, let the hurtful words roll off of you, or seek help from your boss or HR.

Say This:

"Please don't talk to me like that."

"Do you understand how inappropriate that was?"

"Your tone is threatening, and I need you to stop it right now."

"What you're doing is illegal and if you continue harassing me, I will report everything you've been doing to HR."

WHAT NEXT?

If you find relief or resolution from the team tormenter, take a big sigh of relief and then think about how your manager or company might prevent bullying in the future. If you have constructive ideas, schedule time with your boss to discuss. If, no matter what steps you take to put a stop to it, the behavior continues unchecked, start looking for a new job quickly. You've got a lot more to achieve professionally. Don't let this bully get in the way of that.

Chapter 4

ADVANCING YOUR CAREER AND BECOMING THE BOSS

Whether you want to climb the proverbial career ladder and, ultimately, become a manager, director, VP, or even CEO—or you define "career advancement" in other ways—you more than likely aim to continue learning, growing, and developing as a professional. It just feels great when you challenge yourself, evolve, improve, and contribute things that genuinely matter to your employers, your customers, and even the world at large.

Given this, it stands to reason that at some point you'll begin taking some thoughtful steps toward a new job or career, a job with more responsibility (and a bigger paycheck), or a seat on the management team. And then if you do become a boss, you'll need to know how to keep growing individually, while developing a team and navigating the myriad of challenges and responsibilities that come with the territory. That's where this chapter can help.

In this chapter, you'll learn how to determine what advancement looks like for you and how to gain the skills you'll need to succeed going forward. If you're ready to become a leader, you'll find tangible tips that will help you make that transition. And, if you're a newly minted boss (congrats!), you'll gain pointers that'll help you settle in confidently and keep your wits about you as you navigate the most formidable issues managers face.

Remember, personal growth isn't just a nice bonus in life; it's crucial to your overall well-being. So, let's make sure you're ready to prosper professionally.

You're Not Sure of Your Next Career Steps

You're ready for something different, something better, or something *more* in your career...but you have no idea what exactly that something is. Do you want a small promotion or a total change in industry? This is a common challenge among professionals, and one that can be paralyzing if you allow it to be. How do you construct a plan to get you moving forward?

 Try these ideas to address this issue:

1 **Evaluate your top strengths.**
Ask yourself, "What am I really good at and hope to continue doing professionally?" Not sure? Ask people who have seen you in action at work.

2 **Consider the must-have attributes of your next job.**
What do you need in order to feel fulfilled professionally? Autonomy? Prestige? Flexibility? Purpose? Define what matters most so you can evaluate possibilities with this in mind.

3 **Try out your options.**
Rather than guess what a day-in-the-life might be like, reach out to people working in those jobs and ask to shadow them or meet for an informational interview.

4 **Create a plan of action.**
Once you've got a ballpark idea of what's next, assign yourself small tasks that will move you toward that goal.

DON'T BE TOO AFRAID TO MAKE A CHANGE. When considering a career move, it's easy to let fear incapacitate you, especially if you've been conditioned to believe that the wrong move could derail your career entirely. But having a promising idea and doing nothing is far worse than taking a calculated risk and discovering it's not what you wanted after all. Trial and error is how we learn and grow as humans. And, likely, even if you make a misstep, you'll take away valuable skills and lessons. Why not give it a shot?

HERE'S HOW Use these additional tips and questions as you evaluate what comes next for you career-wise.

Think This:

"It's my career: I'm going to take charge!" Just as you will take logistical steps along your career path, you should take mental ones too. Approach your moves with thoughtfulness, goals, and purpose. It's incredibly common for people to let their careers just sort of happen to them versus carving out an intentional path. And while it may all work out, this non-strategy puts you at risk of missing out on an incredible, meaningful career.

Say This:

"If I could wake up tomorrow with my dream job, what would it be?"

"What skills do I need to acquire to be qualified for the job I'd love to have?"

"Who do I need to meet or speak with to learn more about this role?"

"Will I regret it if I don't give this a shot?"

WHAT NEXT?

If you've explored possibilities for your next step and have selected a role, organization, or new field that seems interesting and within reach, build an action plan. You're much more likely to get from point A to point B if you've got a clear road map and actionable steps laid out. If you've determined that what you want is out of reach (for now), it's perfectly okay to pause and decide if you've got the means and determination to make it happen in the long term.

You Want to Find a Mentor to Support Your Career Growth

If you're thinking about finding a mentor, congrats! Plenty of professionals never seek one out, which is unfortunate because having mentors—at any stage of your career—can help you advance more quickly, build relationships with influencers and experts, and—studies show—make more money. So, you're already on the right track. Now, how can you find the right one(s) and make the most out of your time together?

 Try these ideas to address this issue:

1 **Determine your goals.**
Just as you wouldn't show up to an informational interview and simply ask for "information," you shouldn't reach out to a potential mentor with a generic request for "mentorship." Hold off if you don't yet have clarity around your goals.

2 **Spell out why you're asking this person versus someone else.**
Do they have a skill you want to learn, a style you admire, or something else you value? Let them know!

3 **Determine if you should create a formal "ask" for mentorship or ease into it.**
If "Please make this long-term investment in me" feels uncomfortable, start by asking for one meeting and go from there.

4 **Consider asking more than one person for mentorship.**
There's no rule that says you can't have a squad of trusted advisors to help you grow professionally!

DON'T EXPECT THIS TO BE A ONE-WAY DEAL. In fact, that's not a relationship; it's a transaction. While you may very well gain considerable rewards from the wisdom and counsel your mentor provides, think about what you could offer in exchange—and share your thoughts on this as you approach or in the early stages of the relationship. If you're a younger professional, maybe you have a pulse on emerging tools or trends that would be helpful for your mentor to know about. Perhaps they could use a hand on a big project or a fresh perspective. Find ways to make this great for both parties, not just for you.

HERE'S HOW

Here are a few additional things to think about— along with some great starter questions—as you work to find the right mentor.

Think This:	**Say This:**
"I need to choose a mentor carefully." Don't just pick someone because a friend insists on making an introduction or you don't know who else to ask. Think of someone whose personality and values seem to align with yours, who is well-networked, encouraging, and—importantly— reasonably available. When evaluating options, you might even ask yourself the same questions you'd ask if evaluating a love interest: "Are we compatible?" and "Does this have long-term potential?" If yes, go for it!	"I really admire your leadership style and work. Would you be willing to give me a bit of career advice?" "What do you consider your foundational professional values?" "What do you wish you had known about our company (or this field) at my career stage?" "Might you consider meeting on a semi-regular basis?" "How can I support you?"

WHAT NEXT?

If you've scored a supportive and inspiring advisor, congratulations. Now, make sure you're a dream mentee—someone who's grateful and returns the favor however possible. If you find that your mentor isn't as helpful as you'd hoped for, there's no shame in moving on. Thank them for their willingness to support you and keep an eye out for a better match.

You Want to Find a Recruiter to Support Your Job Search

Your former coworker landed a great new job through a recruiter and raved about the experience. As you ponder your next career move, you start thinking that you might want to work with a recruiter too. Unfortunately, you don't know the first thing about finding the right one (and you've heard headhunter horror stories). You're also unsure on how to connect with them once you do. How should you proceed?

 Try these ideas to address this issue:

1 Find someone in your field.
The goal of all recruiters is the same—find great people to fill open jobs. But headhunters vary by type, industry, and area of specialization, so you'll need to find one that's right for you.

2 Decide if you want a permanent position or a contract role.
Some recruiters only fill direct-hire roles; others place people in temp assignments. Ask early on to ensure alignment.

3 Determine if you need an internal or an agency recruiter.
Internal recruiters are employed by one company and fill positions for that one firm (this is a good choice if you've got a dream employer). Agency recruiters represent several companies.

4 Ask around.
Remember that friend who said their experience with a recruiter was great? If they work in a similar job or industry, ask them for an introduction (or contact information).

5 Do a bit of Internet research.
Not sure where to begin? Google "Best recruiting agencies for [your profession] in [your city]."

DON'T SIT AROUND WAITING FOR A RECRUITER TO DIS-COVER YOU. Yes, you may have that one pal who seems to always be getting hit up by recruiters on LinkedIn. But you don't have to simply hang around hoping to be found. If you track down a few headhunters who seem like a good fit for your background and goals, reach out directly to see if your background aligns with their needs. (But still be sure to optimize your LinkedIn profile too. It always feels great when they come to you!)

HERE'S HOW Beyond these initial dos and don'ts, here are a few more ideas to consider and questions to ask as you work to find a recruiter.

Think This:

"This could be a win-win situation." While reaching out directly to recruiters may feel intimidating, consider this: The primary measure of success for any recruiter is how effective they are at filling open positions with great people. So, if you do a bit of legwork in advance—and find a recruiter who's actually looking for people just like you—you may find that they appreciate your outreach, and both of you win!

Say This:

Ask a coworker or friend: "You mentioned that you really liked the recruiter that found you for your new job. Would you be willing to introduce us?"

Ask an agency recruiter: "I'm a robotics programmer. Since your firm seems to specialize in this industry, do you think it might make sense for us to chat?"

Ask an internal recruiter: "Do you work on engineering positions, or would you recommend I speak with someone else on your team?"

WHAT NEXT?

If, after doing your homework and conducting a bit of outreach, you've pinpointed one or more recruiters who seem willing and equipped to work with you, wonderful. Work hard to build a strong and lasting relationship with them. Having a great recruiter among your professional contacts can be enormously helpful throughout your career. If you are hitting dead ends or discovering that a recruiter is unresponsive, don't take it personally. Recruiters are busy and may not always respond to cold outreach. Find another possibility and keep trying!

You Want Feedback on How to Improve Your Work

Even if you're good at what you do professionally, there's always room for improvement. In an ideal environment, you're getting regular feedback on your work, especially from your manager. However, not all bosses are skilled at helping employees develop individually. Likewise, your peers may feel like it's just not their place to offer unsolicited advice. So you may have to be proactive and ask. How do you go about it?

 Try these ideas to address this issue:

1 **Fine-tune your goals—and your specific questions.**
What, exactly, are you looking for in terms of feedback, and what questions should you ask to gather this information?

2 **Ask the right people.**
Yes, your boss is probably a great source of advice, but you surely have respected peers who may also be quite helpful.

3 **Pick your timing and outreach method strategically based on the individual.**
Is this someone who would be fine with a brief meeting, or should you send a few questions via email? Make it easy for them to say yes.

4 **Be ready for whatever comes back.**
When you ask people "How can I improve?" you open yourself up to constructive criticism. Make sure you're emotionally equipped for any observations they may share.

DON'T BE REACTIVE OR GET DEFENSIVE IF ANYONE GIVES YOU NEGATIVE FEEDBACK. It's a vulnerable act—asking someone a question that's tantamount to "Hey, where am I falling short?"—but it's one that may be incredibly worthwhile to your efforts to grow professionally. And, while no one relishes feeling rejected or being given negative feedback, remember that you've asked for their evaluation. Thank them for their candor, then take some time to digest what's been shared instead of reflexively refuting it.

HERE'S HOW

Now that you know the value of asking for feedback—and how to go about it—here's something to think about and some sample talking points for the outreach.

Think This:

"Soliciting others for feedback myself is a better option than waiting for unsolicited advice." In fact, a study by the analytics firm Gallup showed that only 26 percent of employees find this unsolicited guidance helpful, which is understandable. No one likes being pulled aside when they least suspect it. By controlling the timing and approach, you'll be calmer and more open to the feedback being shared.

Say This:

"Could we set up a quick meeting to talk about my progress? I'd love your feedback."

"I'd specifically appreciate your observations on how I'm handling the database project."

"Now that we've got everything wrapped up, I'd love your thoughts on how I did."

"I took your suggestions to heart and revamped the process. What do you think?"

WHAT NEXT?

If you find that, by requesting feedback, you're evolving more quickly than you were before asking for input, share your successes! Certainly, you'll want to loop back around to your advice-giver, but consider telling colleagues how well this approach works too. You may inspire them to follow suit. If you've realized that the input isn't helpful, don't give up. Try fine-tuning the *who* and the *how* you ask. Keep going...and keep growing!

You Feel Prepared to Take On New Responsibilities at Work

You are doing really well at your current job and feeling ready for a fresh challenge. Perhaps you're a bit bored (don't tell your boss this), curious about other areas of the business, or proactively positioning yourself for a future promotion. Whatever your motives, if now feels like the time to explore new horizons at work, take a shot! How do you put together a plan and a pitch and make it happen?

 Try these ideas to address this issue:

1 **Brainstorm possibilities.**
Instead of going to your boss with a basic "I just want more" statement, drum up some specific ideas on what you'd like to take on next.

2 **Prepare a proposal and pitch your idea.**
Be sure to include details on how your employer, team, or boss will benefit if they say yes.

3 **Raise your hand to lead a special project.**
Is the company transitioning to a new payroll processing system (that you know inside and out)? Offer to lead a team in training users on the technology.

4 **Rescue a coworker or team that's struggling.**
If you know of someone who has just piles of work on top of them—and it's something you've got the skills to support them with—offer to pitch in.

DON'T TAKE ON MORE WORK IF YOU CAN'T HANDLE WHAT YOU HAVE NOW. Taking on more responsibilities could very well accelerate your career progression at your company. However, if you're not consistently (and successfully) managing your current workload, now is not the time to ask for new accountabilities or assignments. Make sure you have the skills, the commitment, *and* the bandwidth before making an appeal for more.

HERE'S HOW Use these extra tips and talking points as you ponder and pitch your ideas for further expanding your scope.

Think This:

"I need to be mindful about how I approach this request." Being energetic and driven to accelerate your career is a great thing. But as you embark on your campaign to take on new responsibilities, spend some time thinking about what you really want (not just what's expected of you or of employees in this position) and how the additional work will affect the rest of your life (e.g., your family time or social calendar). Do what's right for all parts of your life.

Say This:

"Since upgrading to the new software version, I've noticed several people fumbling with the new features. May I create and deliver a training for everyone?"

"With tax season coming up, I know the accounting team will be stretched thin. I have some extra time and ideas on how I could help."

"You look overloaded. I know QuickBooks. Can I help?"

WHAT NEXT?

If you can formalize a plan through your manager, that's ideal. By having buy-in, you'll maximize the odds that you'll receive some support as you integrate the new work into your job description. (Plus, they'll see your initiative firsthand!) If your pitch isn't approved, don't let that prevent you from stretching and growing. So long as you don't drop the ball on your expected assignments, you can certainly support others on an informal basis. Or, consider that this company might not have the right opportunities for you in the next phase of your career.

You Want to Demonstrate That You're Ready to Be a Manager

You've decided that you're ready (and eager) to become a manager, but, for whatever reasons, you're not yet in contention for an open spot. Are you supposed to just sort of wait it out, play the game, bide your time? Or are there proactive steps that you can take to make it clear to your manager—and other key decision-makers—that you've got the mindset, initiative, and skills that'll make you a great fit for a leadership role?

 Try these ideas to address this issue:

1 Develop an enterprise-wide mindset.
Good leaders see the big picture and understand the importance of aligning strategy and plans across the organization.

2 Showcase your strong problem-solving skills.
This is what managers do all day long. When you become one, you'll be expected to remove roadblocks, resolve issues, and drive the team toward solutions and success.

3 Gain leadership skills.
You can do this in several ways—volunteer to lead a side project, mentor less-experienced teammates, or take a leadership development course, to name a few.

4 Demonstrate a clear interest in the work (and successes) of others.
This is no time to be endlessly heads-down in your laptop. Great leaders are inspiring, encouraging, and—importantly—available.

DON'T ASSUME THAT THE NUMBER OF YEARS YOU'VE BEEN ON THE JOB AUTOMATICALLY GIVES YOU THE LEG UP WHEN IT COMES TO LANDING A MANAGEMENT ROLE. That's old-school thinking, and it's not how modern organizations fill leadership positions today. Just because you've demonstrated endless loyalty doesn't mean you're management material. You've got to make it clear that you're strategic and empathetic, a strong communicator, and someone with clear potential for developing people and teams.

HERE'S HOW Following, you'll find some situations to ponder and suggested scripts to use when working toward a management role.

Think This:	**Say This:**
"Why do I want to become a manager?" You may want the salary bump or the prestige you envision will come with the territory, but you've also got to be ready and inspired for all the rest of the responsibility that comes with being a boss. Think about the value and unique skills you'll bring to the role and brainstorm how you'll deal with challenges that arise.	"I'll be glad to lead the team in planning the company's fiftieth-anniversary celebration."
	"Would you like for me to meet weekly with the new design engineer to make sure she gets up to speed quickly?"
	"Let's meet with the engineering director before we commit to these changes the client wants. I want to make sure the plan aligns with strategy and is realistic from a design perspective."

WHAT NEXT?

Now, even if you do a great job in demonstrating that you're ready for the next step, it could take a while before you land a management role—for a lot of reasons. If you see a promising pathway at your current company, fantastic. Make your goals known and keep showing up strong. If, however, you're seeing writing on the wall that your employer lacks confidence in your potential for the opportunities that would be right for you—don't give up; just go elsewhere.

You Want to Ask for a Promotion or Raise

Whoever coined the phrase "Never let them see you sweat" surely never asked their boss for a promotion. Making a pitch for a salary bump or more responsibility can make even the most confident person feel nervous. You have to think of what to ask, and how and when to ask it. So if you want to advance your career (and/or bank account), how can you broach the subject?

 Try these ideas to address this issue:

1 **Show your best work well in advance of your request.**
You'll stand the best chance of gaining a yes if you've been showing up every day as a key contributor—one who consistently adds plenty of value and is always willing to go the extra mile.

2 **Be proactive.**
Don't wait for the magical fairy of promotions to arrive or expect that raise to be included in your annual review. Craft a plan, pick a good time, then go after it.

3 **Sell your idea.**
If you're going to take a run at this, do it properly. Collect performance data and feedback from others to support your argument and arrive with a specific and compelling request.

4 **Be ready for any response.**
Surely, "Of course!" is what you're aiming for, but plan for contingencies so you can gracefully respond no matter the reaction.

DON'T OFFER UP ANY ULTIMATUMS AND TRY HARD TO NOT LET EMOTIONS GET THE BEST OF YOU. Even if you're feeling pretty fired up about your situation—perhaps you've been passed by for a raise or promotion before—stay levelheaded. You want to be calm, cool, and collected as you lay out your proposal and highlight your merits. Be sure to focus on the business value you offer now and what's in it for them if they dish up that big, fat raise.

HERE'S HOW

Now that you know what to do and what to bypass, here's a way to frame your mind for the ask, and some potential talking points.

Think This:

"I will be brave and ask for this raise or promotion." Understand that this type of request is nerve-racking for even the most confident and extroverted people among us. It's not you; it's hard. But just because it's hard doesn't mean you shouldn't do it. In fact, the process of preparing for and asking for a promotion or raise—even if unsuccessful—may help you become more confident in your worth and more comfortable advocating for yourself across other aspects of your life.

Say This:

"My client accounts are generating 32 percent of our overall sales revenue and the customer feedback we've received is consistently excellent. Based on this, I am hopeful you will consider bumping my base salary to $75,000."

"I've really enjoyed how my responsibilities have grown to include training new hires. I love the work and my performance rating among students is 98 percent. Based on these successes, would you be open to formalizing my role as training manager?"

WHAT NEXT?

If you've achieved a salary or title bump, give yourself a high five for being your own best promoter...then get to work. Now you need to demonstrate your readiness for the promotion or worthiness of more compensation. If your efforts are unsuccessful, try not to take it personally. More often than not, it's more about current business circumstances than your worth. Decide if there's an alternative pathway to success within your current company or consider building your professional future elsewhere.

You Want to Successfully Advance Your Career While Working from Home

Decades ago, working from home was a rarity. Nowadays, it's more common than ever. Whether you've been working at home for ages or have recently made the transition, you might be wondering how the arrangement will affect your chances at advancement. How can you enjoy the benefits of working from home but still show your worth to your employer?

 Try these ideas to address this issue:

1 **Define "advance" for yourself.**
It's fundamental to know what you want so you can build specific strategies and tactics around that goal.

2 **Be intentional in getting to know people.**
It's common today for virtual coworkers—even those on the same team—to have never met in real life. While an office provides a natural "get to know you" space, when everyone's remote you need to make much more of an effort.

3 **Aim to become indispensable.**
You were hired to add value to the organization, which you're surely doing. The more you can deliver, the more valuable you'll become.

4 **Keep track of your accomplishments.**
You don't want them to fall through the cracks!

5 **Ask for what you want.**
Your boss won't automatically know your career aspirations. Help them help you develop individually as you do great work for the team.

DON'T BE INVISIBLE. This is among the biggest challenges for remote workers, especially those who aren't super comfortable being "on" all the time. Maybe you want to just hunker down and do your work, so you mark yourself as unavailable on Slack. Or you turn your video camera off through meetings. Sure, everyone's going to use these options from time to time. But if you make it a pattern, you'll risk coming off as unengaged or disinterested, which is the opposite of what you're going for.

✔ HERE'S HOW

Now let's focus on what to think and say as you move ahead with your request.

Think This:

"I'm no less valuable as a work-at-home employee." Don't doubt your worth to your employer just because you're not in the office. It can be easy to begin to mentally downplay your success if you're not in the thick of the action in the office, so remind yourself of your skills, accomplishments, and potential as you think about advancing your career. Modern workplaces allow for lots of different paths to success!

Say This:

"I'm looking for some new challenges."

"I noticed a redundancy in our call process and figured out a potential solution. May I share my idea?"

"I'd like to meet to discuss my recent projects and get your input on potential next moves for me career-wise."

WHAT NEXT? ——————————→

If you're intentional and consistent in being visible, available, proactive, and indispensable (no pressure!), you may find this magical combination keeps you very much on the minds of your manager and key influencers. If you fear, however, that you're still being overlooked or forgotten about, ask your boss for suggestions on how you might make more of an impact. Who knows, they may have concrete ideas that you hadn't considered—but that could take you great places within the organization!

You Need a "Manager-Worthy" Resume

You probably already have a resume, and it may have served you quite well in helping you land your current or earlier jobs. But it very likely highlights your skills and strengths as an individual contributor versus those that position you as clear management material. You'll want to add keywords, accomplishments, and information that highlight your skills as a leader. How do you make the transition?

 Try these ideas to address this issue:

1   **Find a few job descriptions that speak to you.**
    If you look closely at the required credentials, you'll see plenty of hints as to what skills, keywords, and experiences you'll want to be sure to highlight.

2   **Provide evidence of your leadership.**
    This may seem like a no-brainer, but you'd be surprised how many people miss this crucial step. If you've managed a project, supervised an intern, or mentored a peer, add that information!

3   **Talk like a leader.**
    Weave in wording that implies leadership. Try these for starters: "strategic thinking," "collaborative," "strong business acumen," "inclusive," "inspiring," "influential." (Peek at those job descriptions again for more hints!)

4   **Nix some entry-level experience from your resume.**
    Remove internships, college GPA, or anything that makes you look rather entry level (unless that information is strategically advantageous to the job you want next!).

DON'T FABRICATE THINGS TO MAKE YOURSELF LOOK MANAGER-WORTHY. Even if you think you'll easily get away with telling the world that you headed up a (make-believe) project or led a (nonexistent) team, misrepresenting yourself is incredibly unethical—and it could catch up with you *years* after the fact. Use the opportunity to put your best foot forward and highlight your capabilities confidently—promoting yourself effectively will go a long way throughout your career. But lying? No way.

HERE'S HOW A few additional thoughts and some phrases to help you prep your resume for your next career chapter.

Think This:	Say This (on Your Resume):
"I should spend some time envisioning myself in a managerial role." How will you lead your employees? How will you handle hiccups like an underperforming worker? What parts of your current job will you no longer be required to (or have time to) complete? Thinking about these topics ahead of time will help you make sure you're highlighting your strengths authentically and strategically. Your goal is to make the "you on paper" as amazing as you in real life!	"Supervised and mentored three engineering interns."
	"Spearheaded and led an innovation initiative."
	"Developed and executed on a strategy that resulted in the firm landing two new clients."
	"Worked collaboratively with business leaders across the organization."
	"Proactively developed curriculum then trained peers on advanced features of Basecamp."

WHAT NEXT? ⟶

If you're successful in shifting your resume messaging from "contributor" to "coach" without outside assistance, consider it a job well done. If you're finding that the task feels a bit daunting, ask for help. Writing about yourself in an impactful way is hard for nearly everyone. If you have the means, find a qualified professional resume writer. If they help you reach your dream job, it'll surely be a worthwhile investment!

You Want to Motivate and Inspire Your Team

Motivating a team is one of the greatest parts of being a manager. Just like a coach on a sports team, you can get the best out of everyone while having fun along the way. You want to be the boss that everyone wants to work for because you're incredible at rallying the troops, known for your passion and energy, and genuinely great at inspiring people to perform at their best. But that is easier said than done. What exactly can you do now to motivate your team and become that leader?

 Try these ideas to address this issue:

1 **Galvanize them around the mission.**
People are far more likely to show up excited and willing to put in the work each day if they feel that they're a part of something bigger than themselves. (Heck, maybe even have a team mantra!)

2 **Give them the tools they need for success, then get out of their way.**
Yes, be there to clear roadblocks, but once they know *what* they need to accomplish, let them determine the *how*.

3 **Be real.**
Just because you're the boss doesn't mean you have to act manager-y all the time. Yes, there's an expected "leader standard" for you, but that doesn't mean you can't be personable and transparent.

4 **Sing their praises at every opportunity.**
Everyone likes to feel valued.

5 **Encourage growth.**
Help them develop individually as they produce great results for the team.

DON'T MICROMANAGE THE TEAM. Having a manager breathing down your neck or nitpicking every little detail about how you work or what you produce is not inspiring at all. In fact, it's very demotivating for virtually every professional. Yes, you will likely have employees that need a little more guidance or supervision than others. But give your people the opportunity to show you what they're made of. They'll appreciate the confidence you have in them.

HERE'S HOW

In addition to the dos and don'ts, here are some additional suggestions to help ensure you're successful in inspiring your team.

Think This:

"Being a successful manager means thinking of the greater good as much as possible." Operating with the mindset that you're this team's fearless leader can help you go to bat for them when it comes to resources, promotions, and raises. While you should still tend to your own needs, putting the team first whenever possible will help you establish yourself as someone who's great to work for.

Say This:

"We've got an important assignment, team. And I know you can carry out the mission!"

"We need to celebrate your successes, team. What an accomplishment!"

"How can I help you reach your goals?"

"Here's where we need to get with this initiative. I know you can pull it off and I'm here if you need my help as you cook up a plan."

WHAT NEXT?

With luck, your efforts to motivate and inspire will come easily and be a resounding success—because you're an absolute natural for the job. But for many people, leadership skills develop over time, with focused attention and experience. So if you feel a bit clumsy or like a novice at first, don't stress about it too much. Keep practicing, seek out motivation and support from those you admire, and remind yourself that you landed this job because people believe you've got what it takes!

You're a First-Time Manager in a Virtual Workplace

Landing your first management role is typically equal parts exciting and nerve-racking. You're moving up, and that's terrific! But there's also so much to learn, so many things to get right (quickly), and often more than a few projects and priorities to juggle right from the start. But what if you're a first-time manager in an environment where everyone is virtual? What are you to do with this extra wrinkle, that is now an incredibly common circumstance?

 Try these ideas to address this issue:

1   **Establish regular communication.**
    One of the biggest risks with virtual teams is that people will feel isolated or forgotten. Find immediate ways to connect regularly with your people across the platforms they're familiar with and use the most.

2   **Be flexible.**
    While there are benefits of working virtually, recognize that it might bring some team members additional challenges. They may have children, roommates, or spouses interrupting them all day, or genuinely miss face time with colleagues. They will appreciate your ability to help them be happy and productive in a way that works for them.

3   **Don't expect to be perfect at this or demand perfection of others.**
    Virtual teamwork can certainly be accomplished, but it's not always easy. Be gentle with yourself and your employees.

4   **Be creative in engaging your people.**
    (And, no, that doesn't just mean another Zoom happy hour.)

DON'T CHANGE TOO MUCH TOO SOON. Generally speaking, change is hard for people, even good change. If your employees aren't entirely used to your management style yet, it's a good idea to assess what's working and what could be improved before you start implementing new procedures. Yes, you should be confident in yourself and excited to take things to the next level. Just be sure to do a temperature check of your team before putting plans in motion.

HERE'S HOW
Here are more suggestions to help you as you get your feet wet as a new manager in a virtual workplace.

Think This:

"What are the potential upsides to managing a team virtually?" You may find that your people are more productive if they don't have to contend with long commutes or daily office interruptions. You'll certainly have access to a dramatically larger pool of candidates if you have zero geographic constraints. And it could be easier for you to uphold a healthy work-life balance if people can fluidly toggle between personal and professional tasks. Focus on the positives even as you manage the challenges.

Say This:

"Outside of our regular team meetings, how do you prefer we communicate?"

"What do you like best about working remotely, and what do you find most challenging?"

"Do you need any training or support on the tools we're using off-site?"

"What feedback do you have on how I'm doing so far?"

WHAT NEXT?

If your team is thriving, that's great. Keep doing what you're doing! But not everyone is cut out for remote work. If you notice a team member struggling, reach out directly and see if you can come up with some creative ideas together that will make that person feel more connected with their job and the overall team. And, if it's possible for your team to—at least occasionally—meet up in person, get that booked. There's nothing quite like face time to build team camaraderie!

You Need to Manage a Conflict Among Your Team Members

Getting in an argument with a sibling or occasionally disagreeing with a longtime pal is just a natural part of life. Conflict happens among people who share time and space, like we do in the workplace. Yet, while it may feel totally doable to resolve personal squabbles, it can be tricky to navigate discord in a professional setting, especially if you're a manager in the middle of a battle among your own team members. How can you manage these difficult situations?

 Try these ideas to address this issue:

1. **Ask yourself, "Can they resolve this on their own?"**
   Ideally, that's a yes, but if you suspect that's unlikely, you're going to need to insert yourself.

2. **Give each team member an opportunity to air their grievances privately.**
   You'll want to get a pulse on each person's position before taking any further actions. Listen actively and investigate if needed.

3. **Bring the group together to express their views and, collaboratively, resolve the issue.**
   Establish ground rules in advance, like "Bring solutions to the discussion" or "No interrupting or name-calling." Work hard to leave this session with a go-forward plan.

4. **Monitor and evaluate progress.**
   Ideally, things get resolved and everyone is happy, but don't assume everything's fine. Keep your eyes peeled so that, if temperatures heat up again, you're ready to douse the fire.

DON'T TAKE SIDES WHEN MANAGING A CONFLICT AMONG TEAM MEMBERS. Your ideal role is that of a mediator—one who helps conflicting parties find their own resolution—versus a judge. If anyone feels that you're playing favorites or not providing an equal opportunity to state their case, you'll likely erode their trust in you and, potentially, exacerbate the situation. Commit yourself to listening objectively and creating a safe environment in which your team members can find resolution.

HERE'S HOW
In addition to the main dos and don'ts, these additional tips will help ensure you're ready to help your team solve the problem.

Think This:	Say This:
"How can this group avoid future feuds and dysfunction?" Are there foundational issues—like lack of a shared purpose or confusion over roles—that need to be addressed? Are you modeling respect and collaboration? Think about any changes you might be able to make to keep the peace in the future.	"Let's meet this afternoon. I'd like to hear your side of the story." "I can tell you're feeling frustrated. Let's get you both together to discuss." "Please bring some ideas on how we can resolve this to the meeting." "I'm checking in to make sure things have improved since we met last week."

WHAT NEXT?

Assuming you're successful in guiding people to resolution, take a few moments to evaluate the conflict after the dust settles. What worked well, and what might you have done better or differently? There's much to learn from challenges like these and, by proactively assessing your performance, you'll grow as a leader. If, however, the situation remains unresolved or escalates, you may need to bring in HR or another support resource. Do whatever it takes to restore the health of your team!

Your Team Is Understaffed

Employees come and go in any organization, and managers quickly become familiar with the hiring process. But when your team is missing key contributors for any stretch of time, performance and morale can take a hit. Managing that in-between time that spans someone's last day and a new hire's start date can be a real challenge. How do you keep people energized and invested when you're low on head count?

 Try these ideas to address this issue:

1 **Lead by example.**
Are your people having to wear many hats right now? If so, this would be a great time to demonstrate your willingness to roll up your sleeves and pitch in wherever needed.

2 **Be transparent about what's going on.**
Share as many details as you can about what's happening and why, and what plans and timelines are for future hiring. (And, if you're hiring now, enlist your people to refer great candidates!)

3 **Recognize those who go above and beyond.**
Burnout is a very real risk when you're running lean. Make sure to express your gratitude regularly and reward those who are keeping things afloat.

4 **Delegate, automate, and outsource.**
If you have some budget wiggle-room, figure out what you can do right now to offload tasks to temps, other teams, or vendors. And, if feasible, deploy technology to save time and reduce manual processes.

DON'T OVERLOOK THE BASICS. When your team is burning the proverbial candle at both ends, it can be easy to let things that aren't urgent slide. But if this means you're shortchanging people on the basic resources they need to get their jobs done—functioning equipment, up-to-date software, relevant data—those smoldering issues may become an inferno in short order. While your demanding customer may yell louder than the decrepit projector in the conference room, they're both likely crucial to keeping the team, and the business, afloat.

✔ **HERE'S HOW** Following are a few more thoughts (and scripts) to support you if your team is understaffed.

Think This:	Say This:
"What things can I control, and what role can I play in bringing in more team members?" Are you hesitant to bring in temps? Painfully slow in interviewing candidates? Certainly, there's likely plenty you can't control, like the larger economy or the employment situation in your local area. But there very well may be things you can (and *should*) do immediately to ease the situation.	"Here's what's going on, and why. Does anyone have any questions?" "Let's brainstorm on how we can stay focused on the most urgent priorities." "You've all been going above and beyond and I want you to know how grateful I am." "These are our most critical-to-fill positions right now. We're offering a $1,000 bonus for anyone who refers candidates who are hired into these roles." "I'm going to roll up my sleeves and help get us through this. What can I do?"

WHAT NEXT? ⟶

If you've implemented measures that help alleviate the immediate issue, great. Now try to identify ways to mitigate risk of similar scenarios down the road. Do you need to implement a faster recruitment process? Should you automate tasks? If company higher-ups won't let you hire new employees to fill the roles, consider making a strong pitch to leadership for relief—or turn your focus to land a new job.

You Want to Retain Your Top-Performing Employees

It's every manager's dream to assemble an amazing, invested, and high-performing team. But bringing talented people into the organization isn't the end-all; you've got to keep your employees—especially your superstars—challenged, inspired, and motivated so they'll keep doing great work and, importantly, stick around for a long time. Retaining your best people isn't easy—people have high standards, and they may have options. So, how can you convince your heavy hitters to stay?

 Try these ideas to address this issue:

1 **Create a purpose-driven environment.**
   People want to feel that their work is meaningful and their efforts are contributing to a larger purpose.

2 **Encourage feedback, and make sure everyone feels safe sharing it.**
   By creating an environment in which team members know their input isn't just welcome—but crucial—you'll demonstrate to them that they're vital to the organization.

3 **Provide flexibility.**
   Offering flexible hours or work arrangements isn't just a nice gesture; it typically improves performance.

4 **Recognize them publicly.**
   Humans want to be seen, to be valued, to be heard. When you acknowledge the contributions of an employee, you'll motivate them to keep up the great work.

5 **Invest in their growth and development.**
   By enabling top performers to continue learning, they won't see leaving as their only option for continued growth.

DON'T DUMP ALL YOUR WORK ON YOUR BEST EMPLOY-EES. There's no doubt that high-performing employees are more productive than their peers, but your star players aren't immune to burnout nor are they unaffected when they feel they're being taken for granted. So be sure you're not piling on the work or calling on a top performer to deal with the toughest issues (because you know they can handle it)—and not acknowledging their efforts or offering extra pay or downtime.

HERE'S HOW In addition to the tangible tips just outlined, here's something to contemplate—and a few scripts to support you.

Think This:

"I can't make everything perfect all the time, despite my best intentions." You may feel pressured to make things hassle-free at all times for your top performers, but your best people aren't looking for a completely perfect workplace from you. They're looking for authenticity, trust, transparency, purpose, and respect. Spend time creating pathways for success, not chasing the impossible.

Say This:

"How can I help you develop professionally?"

"I trust you to work through this challenge without my looking over your shoulder, but I'm right here if you need support as you move forward."

"We need to make some big-picture decisions and I'd love your input."

"You really knocked it out of the park on this project. I'm going to make sure management knows how you've contributed."

WHAT NEXT?

With thoughtful leadership, overall company support, and a little luck, you'll be able to keep your top performers engaged, happy, and fulfilled. If, despite your best efforts, you're still struggling to keep your top talent, ask someone (within your company or outside of it) with a record of success in retaining great people what their secret is. Above all, remember that sometimes people move on because of circumstances beyond your control. Try to keep your relationship friendly—you never know when your paths might cross again.

You Want to Reassure Employees During a Difficult Time

Unfortunately, every business hits a difficult point at one time or another. Whether it's specific to your company (maybe you've been bought out), your industry (maybe technology is rendering some of your products obsolete), or the world at large (geopolitics affecting the stock market), you might be leading a team that's anxious, unsure, or even afraid. As a manager, your ability to remain calm and functional in the workplace is key. How can you reassure your team through rough stretches?

 Try these ideas to address this issue:

1 **Be transparent.**
If the stressors are related to something impacting the company, be honest with your team about what's going on, and update them regularly.

2 **Stay positive.**
Sure, it may be challenging to do so, especially if the issues are impacting you directly as well. But try hard to be the optimistic calm in the storm for your team.

3 **Provide or point employees to self-care or support options.**
Give everyone an extra day of PTO, remind them about the employee assistance program (if you have one), or bring in a helpful speaker. Do everything you can to preserve your team's emotional wellness.

4 **Cut them some slack.**
Approve their request to finish the project over the weekend (assuming deadlines permit), or to cut out early on Fridays for now.

DON'T MAKE PROMISES THAT YOU SIMPLY CANNOT KEEP.
Sure, it may be tempting to say, "You aren't going to lose your job" or "We'll be able to rearrange your schedule to make this work." But if you don't know with certainty that this is possible, keep your lips zipped until you have confirmation. If you don't, you may ultimately damage trust, and that's mighty hard to restore once the deed is done. You can still be encouraging and empathetic without overselling what you can actually do.

HERE'S HOW A few more things to consider and say when you need to reassure your team.

Think This:

"I need to check in with my own mental health during this time." Do you need to rest and recharge? You likely are experiencing some of the same difficult emotions as your employees, and it's okay to address them—and communicate some of them to your team if you want. Sharing thoughts like "I'm feeling uneasy about this situation too" or "Whew, I need to take a break and clear my head" shows your team that you're caring for your own well-being as well as theirs.

Say This:

"What are your top concerns right now?"

"What questions can I answer about what's happening?"

"What specific things can I do to help you feel supported through this?"

"Do you have suggestions that may be helpful for the team right now?"

"What ways do you find most helpful when you're trying to manage stress?"

WHAT NEXT? ⟶

If you're able to keep your team relatively calm, informed, and motivated during this tough time, kudos. Leading teams through a fire is hard work, and your employees will no doubt appreciate all that you've done for them. If your team's productivity declines dramatically or there's no end in sight to this difficult situation, you might need to take things to the next level and ask your HR department for more structured support.

You Have to Fire Someone

There's plenty of great things about being a manager. But you'll also likely find there are some less-than-savory aspects of being in charge—including having to fire people. Whether it's your first time or you've done it before, it's typically enormously difficult news to deliver. But it's a necessary part of the job, so how can you get it right?

 Try these ideas to address this issue:

1 Make sure you're following policy—and the law.
Review your company handbook and/or meet with HR to make sure you're doing this the right way.

2 Have someone else in the room with you, preferably HR.
They'll calm your nerves and support you as you deliver the news. Likewise, they'll eliminate any potential "he said, she said" legal scenarios.

3 Get right to the point.
It's easy to babble when you're nervous or feeling guilty, but this only drags out the inevitable.

4 Show empathy, but don't waffle.
Your employee needs to see that you care, but also know without a shadow of a doubt that their employment is ending.

5 Allow them time to process the news in private.
Likewise, try to give them some time and space to collect their things, return company equipment, and, if possible, gracefully say goodbye to their colleagues.

DON'T FIRE SOMEONE IMPULSIVELY amid a heated disagreement or to punish them for something they dropped the ball on. No matter how contentious your relationship with a team member, or how egregious the circumstances behind the termination, acting too impetuously could backfire. You need to collect your thoughts, your evidence, and your support staff to ensure you're not opening the company up for potential legal recourse. Keep your emotions in check, and work through this in a polished and professional manner.

HERE'S HOW
Use these tips and scripts as you prepare for "the talk" with your employee.

Think This:	Say This:
"Firing people is part of the job." You may feel sad, guilty, or nervous if you have to fire someone. That's natural, and a sure sign that you're a caring and empathetic person. But as a manager, you'll need to accept that it's your responsibility. Think about how you'd like to be notified if tables were turned, and try to do that. And then, take a little breather to clear your head before you dive back into work.	"You're being terminated and here's why."
	"I'm sorry, but we've lost funding for your role. Your last day will be Friday."
	"I'm willing to answer your questions. And you're welcome to vent if you'd like, but that won't change our decision."
	"Would you prefer to leave now and have us ship your things to you next week?"

WHAT NEXT? ⟶

If the termination goes smoothly, quietly commend yourself for managing through an incredibly difficult task professionally and humanely. If things go a bit sideways, get through the immediate situation then reflect on how you could have done things differently or better. You may need to let someone go again in the future, so take the time to fine-tune your approach (even as you hope it's a very long time before you've got to go through it again!).

Your Employees Don't Respect You

Landing a management role is something that typically comes with a lot of pride—and certain expectations. As the boss, you surely expect your team to be engaged and inspired to produce their best work. You may also assume that your position of authority will command their respect. Unfortunately, respect isn't given, it's earned. And if you're not earning it, it won't be just your ego that takes a hit; it'll be the performance and morale of your entire team. How can you turn things around if your employees don't respect you?

 Try these ideas to address this issue:

1   **Seek out feedback and make it safe for your team to share it.**
    Pull people aside one by one and ask for their honest feedback on what you could do better. It may be hard to hear, but you need to hear it. Thank them for sharing and then take their input to heart.

2   **If you know you've made a mistake, admit it.**
    Own up to your shortcomings, then let your team know what you'll do going forward to avoid making a similar blunder.

3   **Get into the trenches with your team, especially when a project merits "all hands on deck."**
    People want to work for leaders who will stand shoulder to shoulder with their teams to ensure success.

4   **Communicate better.**
    Be as transparent as you can. Listen actively. Update the team regularly. Be available. *Care.* Strong communication skills are at the very top of the list for commanding respect as a leader.

DON'T FLIP RIGHT INTO CONFRONTATION OR DISCIPLINARY MODE IF YOUR TEAM DOESN'T RESPECT YOU. While you may be feeling a bit hurt or even angry about the situation, it's best not to retaliate (unless, of course, this is a chronic issue with an employee you've already set expectations with). If your employees are feeling disrespected, ignored, or even abused by you (which may be why they don't respect you), you'll never correct the situation by being heavy-handed.

✓ HERE'S HOW Here are a few more things to think about or say as you work to get to the bottom of the issue.

Think This:

"I might need to self-reflect." Beyond your team's feedback (which may be limited, especially if they don't care enough to open up to you) and tangible tactics to "fix" the situation, a bit of self-reflection (or advice from a trusted ally) may be useful if you're feeling disrespected. Are you coming across as unavailable or unappreciative of their efforts? Do you close your door to avoid hard conversations? Do you remove roadblocks for them—or are you maybe one? How can you improve *you* as you fix the problem?

Say This:

"I see the work you put into this, and I really appreciate it."

"I know my unavailability has made things hard on the team. Here's what I plan to do going forward."

"I'm feeling a bit disrespected of late. Let's meet as a team and talk about what's going on."

"I made a mistake. I'm sorry."

WHAT NEXT? ⟶

With patience and leading by example, you might be able to gain your team's respect. If your efforts don't reap immediate rewards, though, don't panic. This may very well take some time. Be consistent, be calm, and demonstrate that you're invested in the team and committed to the health of the group. If it's obvious that you've got one or two toxic employees—who are effectively poisoning the entire team—you may need to weed them out so the group can, ultimately, thrive.

You Are Significantly Younger Than Everyone Else on Your Team

When someone suggests that age is just a number, perhaps they've never been called upon to manage a team of much older employees. (Can you say "intimidating"?) But even if you're worried about managing people who are several decades older than you, here's the thing to remember: You were chosen to be the boss. Your employer knew you're worthy of that seat. So, how can you put your best foot forward right from the start?

 Try these ideas to address this issue:

1 **Be confident and humble.**
Your team does need to understand that you know your stuff. But it'll also go a long way if they see that you're not cocky or arrogant about it.

2 **Learn from them.**
Demonstrate your enthusiasm for the opportunity to tap in to the knowledge of others on your team and the perspectives of those who have traveled paths you've not yet encountered.

3 **Be friendly but authoritative.**
While it's understandable that you want to cultivate an engaged team and manage employees who think you're both inspiring and *fun*, remember that you're not there to be their buddy. You're there to lead the group and help each employee grow professionally while delivering their absolute best for the team.

DON'T CHANGE EVERYTHING RIGHT OFF THE BAT. Pace yourself. While you may very well have incredible ideas on how to modernize, optimize, or reshape the team, ease into any big changes. These employees may be quite comfortable with "how we've done things" and proud of what they've built. Be sure you know the ins and outs of processes and procedures and gain your employees' respect and trust before you implement your transformations.

✓ HERE'S HOW

Aside from the basics, use these tips and scripts to succeed as the much-younger manager of a team.

Think This:	**Say This:**
"It's best not to dwell on things I can't change." Instead, focus your energy on what you can do. One of the challenges of being a younger boss is that you likely have relatively little experience as a manager. There's no changing your age or number of years you've been in the workforce, of course. But what you do have some control over is how quickly you gain or strengthen skills needed to be effective at your job. Think about how you can develop yourself as you embark on developing others.	"You are truly the expert on our current software system. Would you be willing to share your knowledge through this software migration?" "What are some of the reasons you've stayed with the company over the years?" "Is there anything you miss about your earliest years?" "You're great at mentoring new hires. I appreciate your willingness to help them learn the ropes."

WHAT NEXT? ——————————————————————→

As you ease into your role, make it easy for people to experience the perks of having a younger boss—fresh ideas, complementary skills, and a willingness to learn from you, to name a few. If you can set a foundation of mutual appreciation and respect right away, chances are everyone will come to find the dynamic mutually beneficial. If, however, you have team members who simply won't put the age difference aside, remember: You're the boss. Respond accordingly.

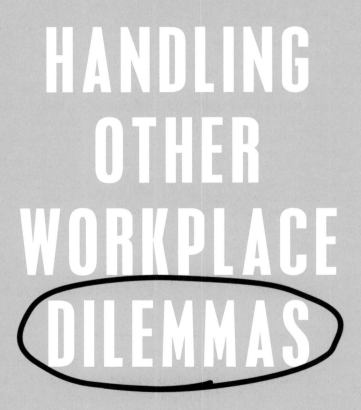

Chapter 5

HANDLING OTHER WORKPLACE DILEMMAS

No matter what level you're at professionally—just starting out, trying to make the most of your final career chapter, or somewhere in the middle—you're going to run into unexpected challenges: A client will get on your last nerve. A family member will be in crisis. You'll goof something up. Or, perhaps, you'll start feeling run-down, underqualified, or even like you've picked the wrong profession entirely.

And while you may feel like the only person on earth dealing with that particular issue when it surfaces, you might be relieved to hear you're not alone. Nearly every working professional faces myriad workplace dilemmas throughout their careers. Challenges and setbacks, as aggravating as they may be, are simply part of everyone's career arc.

This is not to say, however, that your only option is to wallow around passively in that inevitable adversity. While you should absolutely allow yourself to feel your emotions, vent to those who will listen, and let go of anything you cannot control, you've got plenty of options when it comes to managing and resolving most professional predicaments.

After reading this chapter, you'll be prepared to tackle some of the most common and formidable issues that people come up against in the workplace. You'll know how to advocate for yourself if you're experiencing bias or burnout, come to terms with a layoff or demotion, own up to errors, and weigh options if you're feeling an itch for something different. These power-packed lessons just might save the day for you today, tomorrow, or five years from now.

You Discovered Your Coworker (in the Same Job) Makes Considerably More Than You

You're just dropping off the documents your teammate left on the scanner when you knock some paperwork on the floor. Bending down to grab it, you see it's their pay stub. You didn't *intend* to read it, but, well, you had to pick it up. In a split second, you went from blissful ignorance to sharp awareness that your coworker—who has the *exact same job* as you—makes a lot more than you. Now what?

 Try these ideas to address this issue:

1. **Make sure this is *really* an apples-to-apples comparison.**
   Are you both adding equitable value? Do you share similar prior experience and skills? Try looking at things objectively before doing anything rash.

2. **Meet with your manager to discuss a raise (but make it about your performance versus your discovery).**
   If you feel strongly that your work merits additional compensation, build a convincing argument and pitch it to your boss. (See the "You Want to Ask for a Promotion or Raise" entry in Chapter 4 for ideas.)

3. **Investigate if the discrepancy violates any federal or state laws.**
   There are laws on the books that prohibit wage discrimination based on gender, race, age, national origin, or disabilities. If you strongly suspect this to be the case, bone up on laws that protect you or find an attorney specializing in employment law.

DON'T RESPOND WHILE YOU'RE STILL PROCESSING THE INITIAL SHOCK. No matter how demoralized, depressed, or outraged you may feel upon discovering your colleague makes more than you, it's best to collect information and thoughts before saying anything. An impulsive outburst may damage your relationship with your manager and coworker(s). Likewise, don't confront your coworker. It's not *their* fault they're more highly compensated than you. It's also not their issue to fix.

HERE'S HOW Here are extra pointers and scripts that'll help as you evaluate your options and activate a plan to level the paycheck playing field.

Think This:	**Say This (to Your Boss to Reach Equal Compensation):**
"This situation could be a bummer for me—but still be justifiable." While every state in the US outlaws wage discrimination (based on varying criteria), your colleague may earn more for reasons that are perfectly fair and legal. For instance, they may have more tenure or could have started their job when the market demand dictated a higher salary. They could have more specialized skills than you or perform at a higher level. You probably don't know the specific factors behind the discrepancy, so consider that this could be a tough situation that you can't change quickly.	"I'm very motivated to be a top performer for the team and the company. I'm hopeful you'll give me a raise based on my achievements from this past year." "I've researched salary ranges. Based on that research and my performance, would you consider giving me a $10,000 raise?" "May I share data from my three biggest wins and customer feedback from these projects?"

WHAT NEXT? ⟶

If your performance aligns with your coworker's—and your manager has room in the budget—you might get that raise. If your boss says you'll have to wait until your next performance review (or the end of a hiring freeze, or whatever)—or flat-out denies your request—you'll need to decide if you're willing to keep bringing your A game to work in spite of the discrepancy. If not, take that A game to a company that recognizes your worth.

You Are Struggling to Prioritize or Stay Organized

Not everyone is a natural-born organizer. Most of us don't learn organizational skills while growing up, and we have different tolerance thresholds when it comes to disarray. Whatever the reasons, if you're finding it challenging to stay organized, you should find some tools and solutions fast—because virtually *all* jobs come with an expectation that you'll prioritize tasks proficiently and meet deadlines. How can you get your tasks in order?

 Try these ideas to address this issue:

1   **Be realistic about how long tasks will take.**
    Do you find yourself saying, "Oh, I can get that done in 20 minutes" but then needing an hour? If so, set a timer and see how long it *really* takes you to get things done.

2   **Set milestone deadlines for yourself.**
    If you feel overwhelmed every time you look at a big project, break it into smaller chunks and assign completion dates for each piece.

3   **Limit interruptions.**
    Close the door, mark yourself as "busy" online, set an out-of-office message. Do what's needed to stay focused.

4   **Find the right organizational tools, or start using the ones your company already offers.**
    There are so many amazing software options today—Trello, Google Docs, Evernote, Asana, Outlook, the list goes on. If technology overwhelms you, ask someone in IT to assist.

5   **Ask for help.**
    We're not all good at all things. Don't flounder; ask your boss for support.

DON'T DEPLOY ORGANIZATIONAL SYSTEMS OR METHODS THAT YOU WON'T USE ROUTINELY JUST BECAUSE OTHER PEOPLE LIKE OR RECOMMEND THEM. If you pick a software platform that feels too complicated or just doesn't feel like something that's going to work for you, you might find yourself more overwhelmed than you were in the first place. Set yourself up for success and find the solutions that meet your needs and your work style.

✓ HERE'S HOW
Taking things beyond the basics, here's something else to ponder, and a few questions to ask yourself and those around you.

Think This:

"How do I work best?" (Do you need your priority list to be super structured? Are you highly visual? Are you technology averse?) Then try out an organizational method or two that feel like a fit. There's no one perfect method for prioritizing or staying organized—people are all different. Also, instead of focusing on surface-level things like nice-looking gadgets or colorful spreadsheets, think about what will truly help you stay on task.

Say This:

Ask yourself: "What am I struggling with? What methods might align with how I work and think?"

Ask your buddy in IT: "Are there tools the company offers that might help me stay on track with deliverables?"

Ask your ultra-efficient teammate: "Your Slack conversations look so organized. Can you show me how you did that?"

Ask your manager: "Would you help me prioritize my projects?"

WHAT NEXT? ⟶

If you find success with certain processes, methods, and/or technology tools, fabulous. Now document it. That's right: Write down the specific things you've found to be most useful in helping you stay organized. This way, should you find yourself struggling again down the road, you can revisit—and fine-tune—your approach. If you've tried some options but not yet found the right formula, don't give up. Keep exploring like your career depends on it, because it truly does.

You Make a Major Mistake

People make mistakes at work every single day. Of course we do; we're human. And most often, our office blunders are small(ish) and forgivable—we forget to return a call, we jam the shredder, or we're late for the team meeting (again). Every now and again, however, someone makes a huge—possibly even job-threatening—error. And, if that someone happens to be you, it's going to feel awful. And you're going to need to act fast. What should you do?

 Try these ideas to address this issue:

1 **Take some deep breaths.**
You're going to be best equipped to respond to your wrongdoing if you can keep yourself at least semi-calm.

2 **Be accountable.**
Alert your manager immediately. Own the mistake, apologize, and—importantly—come with ideas on how you'll make amends.

3 **Be ready for the fallout.**
Depending on the error, you may have a lineup of people fuming at you. Steel yourself for these reactions—and know it may take some time to get yourself back into people's good graces.

4 **Evaluate what you've learned from the situation.**
You might be able to use it as an opportunity for growth.

5 **Proceed in a manner that makes it clear that you're committed to fixing things or doing better.**
Don't just tell people what you'll do differently; *show* them.

DON'T LIE, TRY TO COVER UP YOUR MISTAKE, OR ATTEMPT TO PASS BLAME ALONG TO SOMEONE ELSE. Any one of these decisions has a high probability of backfiring on you and—depending on the transgression—could do a lot more damage than the error itself to your career, your reputation, and the overall organization. Unless you've made a (literal) life-or-death misstep, there are probably several constructive responses that will improve the state of affairs if you own up immediately and get moving on making any possible repairs.

✔ HERE'S HOW Here is something to ponder and a few things to say as you work through a major mistake.

Think This:	**Say This:**
"This feels so heavy, but I need to try keeping things in perspective." Will anyone die from this? Probably not. Will people lose trust in you *forever*? Assuming you're actively working toward earning it back, that's doubtful. It's so easy to jump to the worst-case scenario when you're feeling panicked, but rarely does that scenario pan out. Be accountable, sure. But be kind to yourself in the process.	"I've made a mistake and wanted to alert you of the situation right away." "It was an honest mistake, but I know it's not a small one. I'm so sorry. Here's what I intend to do to minimize the impact." "How else can I improve this situation or make things right?" "I'm committed to earning back your trust."

WHAT NEXT? ⟶

Assuming your client, manager, coworker—whoever was negatively impacted—forgives you, do yourself a favor and forgive yourself too. Yes, you may need to have some uncomfortable conversations and take things a day at a time, but reliving the mistake for all eternity will serve no one. And even if they can't get past the transgression? Forgive yourself anyway. Then press on with a great, albeit difficult, life lesson under your belt.

You Are Put On a Performance Improvement Plan

A performance improvement plan (PIP) is a written plan designed to help underperforming employees improve their skills and performance. It outlines developmental milestones and expected improvements and sets a date for re-evaluation. Many firms issue PIPs as an alternative to firing someone. Though it's meant to help you, the process can be stressful, especially if you didn't see it coming. No one likes being called out for their shortcomings. It's even worse when done in this incredibly official and potentially livelihood-impacting manner. How can you deal?

 Try these ideas to address this issue:

1 **Read it carefully.**
You need to know exactly what's expected of you and in what time frame.

2 **Let your emotions settle before doing anything.**
Don't panic. PIPs happen. And, while it's *possible* your employer is using the PIP to cover their bases before firing you, most managers have good intentions and hope the PIP will help you get back on track.

3 **Decide if you agree with the assessment and are willing to put in the effort.**
If you think that it's just not going to be worth it, consider resigning. However, if you feel the job's worth saving, proceed with a solid plan *and* a positive attitude.

4 **Keep your manager updated on your progress.**
Being proactive will work in your favor.

5 **Ask for help.**
When you get a PIP, let go of your pride and reach out to people around you for help.

✓ HERE'S HOW

Now that you've dealt with the initial receipt of the PIP, here are more things to consider and say.

Think This:	Say This:
"I need to be gentle with myself." It is very easy to get down on yourself when you receive feedback like this, but losing all of your confidence and motivation won't help you right the ship. Focus on what you can control, remind yourself of your many talents and skills, and adopt a mindset of personal growth. You'll likely come out of the process a stronger employee, and you should celebrate your resilience and dedication.	"Can you clarify what this means? I want to make sure I have a clear understanding of your expectations." "I appreciate your giving me this opportunity. I won't let you down." "Would you be willing to help me with _____ as I get started?" "Here's a progress report from the past week. Do you have any feedback for me?"

WHAT NEXT? ⟶

If you are able to complete your PIP goals by the deadline, give yourself a pat on the back (way to persevere!). Then request a meeting with your manager to discuss how you can ensure you're never in that situation again. If you make it through the plan period but find your boss is still unsure of your work or micromanaging your every move, solicit their honest feedback. You may not love what they say, but it'll help you decide where you go from there. If they remain unconvinced of the quality of your work, you can decide whether to keep trying to impress them or find a new job.

You Are Dealing with a Major Family Issue

Juggling work *and* a significant family issue is physically exhausting and emotionally draining. Can you really be expected to keep pace with that market research or data analysis when your mom just had a stroke, or you're getting divorced? Trying to manage two important parts of your life when one is in upheaval is extremely difficult, so be easy on yourself during this time. How can you do your best to get through it?

 Try these ideas to address this issue:

1. **Decide if you're going to tell anyone at work.**
   Will the issue likely be resolved quickly or is this long term? Is it impacting your work? Will you feel better if you talk it out? There's no single answer when it comes to disclosure. Weigh your options and decide what's best for you.

2. **If you tell your manager, be sure to spell out what you need.**
   Do you need to work from home for a while? Part-time hours? A quiet conference room for Zoom calls with a loved one? Be specific.

3. **Do your best to keep up with the workload.**
   Don't forget to keep your boss and team updated on your projects.

4. **If it's just too much to try to continue working, research short-term leave options.**
   You may be entitled to up to twelve weeks of unpaid leave thanks to the federal Family and Medical Leave Act (FMLA).

DON'T DRIVE YOURSELF TO THE POINT OF SHEER EXHAUSTION. That may be nearly impossible, and you understandably won't want to let anyone down. But your family members need you right now. And, yes, your employer does too, but in a much different way. If you're trying to be everything to everyone day upon day, you'll run a high risk of burnout. You won't be very useful to anyone if you're not taking care of yourself.

✔ HERE'S HOW

Aside from the main dos and don'ts, here's something more to think about—and a few potential talking points.

Think This:

"My two most powerful tools are patience and routine." Patience will help you stay focused on the big picture rather than unraveling over the smaller concerns that will surely arise. And maintaining as much of a routine as possible will enable you to feel calmer and in control, even when your life is a roller coaster. Remind yourself that these difficult times do eventually pass, and be sure you are getting whatever support you need.

Say This:

"The prognosis looks good, but I'll need two hours off every Tuesday for her treatment. Can that be arranged?"

"Will you consider cutting my hours in half for the next eight weeks?"

"I appreciate your care and concern, but I'd rather not discuss the details."

"How about I update you on work projects once a week, so you know where I'm at with things?"

WHAT NEXT?

If your manager approves a plan that allows you to keep work obligations afloat while undergoing the rigors of the family situation, thank them for their understanding and make the most out of your time on the job. If they won't cut you any slack, or you discover the concessions aren't enough, think hard about taking that leave (or resigning). It may be tough in the short term, but family issues should take precedence.

You Suspect Ageism at Work

Open any lifestyle magazine. Scroll through your *Instagram* feed. You'll see it everywhere you look—the loud and clear message that looking, acting, and *being* youthful is prized above most everything in our culture. It's no wonder, then, that so many older adults encounter ageism—the act of being treated unfairly or negatively stereotyped based on your age—at work. In fact, a recent AARP survey shows that nearly 80 percent of older workers report having seen or experienced it at work. If that includes you, what next?

 Try these ideas to address this issue:

1 **Examine your own sensitivities first.**
If you know that you're acutely uncomfortable about aging, you might be highly sensitive to anything related to your age. Try to look at the situation objectively or ask a trusted friend to weigh in.

2 **Go on the offense.**
Brainstorm what you can control about this situation. Of course you can't jump into a time machine, but what can you do to come across as energetic, curious, and current?

3 **Confront the offender.**
If someone is singling you out for your age, call it out! If you think it was unintentional, broach the matter gently, of course, but shine some light on the situation.

4 **Document repeat offenses.**
If it's a pattern, report it to your boss or HR. You may also consider filing an EEOC complaint. Age discrimination has been illegal in the US since 1967.

DON'T COP AN ATTITUDE TOWARD EVERYONE YOUNGER THAN YOU. When you view your younger colleagues as the collective enemy, you're bound to treat them with negativity or resistance. If you adopt an "everyone younger is out to get me" mindset, you risk unfairly mistreating others and earning a reputation as negative and set in your ways. Embracing the opportunity to thrive in a multigenerational workplace is important for anyone.

HERE'S HOW
Here's one more thing to think about, and a few questions to ask if you suspect age discrimination at work.

Think This:

"Can I flip the script on this topic and show my boss, clients, and coworkers how my combined skills and experience provide me with an unstoppable combination of superpowers?" Try thinking about the benefits of your age (e.g., years of experience, maturity, etc.) in tandem with what could be considered your more "youthful" traits, like energy, curiosity, and innovative thinking. By demonstrating that you offer the best of both worlds, you may well find peace with your age—and silence the critics.

Say This:

Ask yourself: "Why do I think this is age discrimination?"

Ask the offender: "Can you help me understand why you said/did that?"

Ask your boss: "I've noticed a pattern of treatment that I want to speak with you about."

Ask Human Resources: "I've documented several instances of ageism that I'd like to share with you."

Ask a lawyer or the EEOC: "I would like to see if I have an age discrimination case here."

WHAT NEXT?

If you can find a way to feel at ease at work and continue thriving professionally as you age, you're in a great spot. Work may just be your golden ticket in keeping you challenged, intellectually stimulated, and cognitively sharp throughout the aging process. If, however, you're in an environment that clearly devalues older workers, see if you can make the situation right—and if that doesn't work, find a new job.

You Get Demoted

"We're moving you into another role" is music to your ears if you're getting promoted. If, however, you're being reassigned to a role with a lower title, fewer responsibilities, and/or less money, it sounds a lot different. Being demoted is among the more demoralizing experiences you can go through in your career, especially if you didn't see it coming, or it's the talk of the office, or both. How can you keep your head held high?

 Try these ideas to address this issue:

1 **Make sure you understand exactly what's happening, and why.**
Is this performance related? Is your role being eliminated? Is the company struggling financially? Get the complete scoop, in writing, ASAP.

2 **Catch your breath before responding.**
This news will likely knock the wind out of you. If you're unable to discuss things calmly right away, ask for time to digest.

3 **Decide what you'll do.**
Do you refocus, regroup, and stay? Do you stay only until you find a new job? Or do you outright quit? There's no correct answer to this; pick the direction that seems best for you given the circumstances.

4 **Update your resume.**
Given the precariousness of the situation, you should be ready for action no matter what you decide right now.

DON'T IMMEDIATELY QUIT. While you may be tempted to tell your boss exactly how you feel about the demotion then storm out (dramatically), think twice about quitting on the spot. Why? For starters, burning bridges is *never* a wise idea. You never know how or when former managers or colleagues could provide a reference or reappear later in your work life. Also, it may be easier (and quicker) to find a new job if you're still employed through the search.

HERE'S HOW Are you being, *ahem*, reassigned? Here's a way of thinking about it, and a few talking points.

Think This:

"I need time to process these difficult feelings." You may find it useful to allow yourself time to fully digest this blow to your ego and step through the common stages of grief: denial, anger, bargaining, depression, and acceptance. Your confidence is surely bruised; you might be scared about the financial aspect of it, fuming mad, or feeling incredibly let down.

Say This:

"This is admittedly disappointing. Can you help me understand exactly why this is happening?"

"Is there anything I can do to move back into a higher position? If so, can we set a plan?"

"If I agree to this, I want to ensure I'm fully committed. May I think about it for a day or two?"

WHAT NEXT?

If you've come to terms with being demoted, it's time to dedicate yourself to your new role. Do your best to stay positive and share your progress and wins with your manager regularly. (If they see that you're resilient and a true team player, it may pay off going forward!) If you've considered it thoughtfully but just can't accept this new position, it's perfectly fine to move on. This hiccup on your career path doesn't have to dictate your whole professional future.

You Get Laid Off

Getting laid off—even when you see it coming—is an incredibly distressful experience. In a flash, you go from having a job, an office, an income, and—for many—an *identity*, to swimming in a sea of uncertainty. And, even if you understand that this isn't your fault, you work in a field with plenty of opportunity, or you've made a successful comeback from a layoff before, figuring out what to do next can be tricky. What moves should you make?

 Try these ideas to address this issue:

1 **Hit pause.**
Even if you need to find another job urgently, take time to process your emotions. Grieve, vent, yell into your pillow, or clear your head before doing anything reactive.

2 **Close out thoughtfully.**
Figure out your options for benefits, see if a severance package or outplacement support is available, collect your final paycheck or bonuses, and ask your employer for a favorable reference.

3 **File for unemployment benefits ASAP.**
You want to start receiving payments right away!

4 **Freshen up your brand, and your paperwork.**
Once you've decided on what you want, make sure your messaging—in your resume, LinkedIn profile, and cover letter—positions you as a strong fit for the jobs you're targeting.

5 **Spread the word.**
Let your friends, family members, and professional contacts know what you're looking for, and ask them to make introductions or pass along leads if they hear of anything.

DON'T GO IT ALONE. It can be tempting to suffer in silence out of sadness or embarrassment, but that's a mistake for several reasons. Your friends and loved ones can provide you with a shoulder to cry on or the listening ear you need as you process the initial emotions. Your professional contacts may provide valuable advice, make introductions, or even know of an open position you'd qualify for. There is absolutely no shame in losing one's job; trust that your people will rally around you through the transition.

✓ HERE'S HOW
Use these additional ideas and talking points if you've been laid off.

Think This:	Say This:
"Maybe this change will turn out to be a blessing for some reason." Try to find the silver lining in your situation, even if that takes a bit of time to have that perspective. You could find a job with a much easier commute. Maybe your next position will pay more. Or, it could be the perfect opportunity to think outside the box—go back to school, open your own business, or change industries.	"Can you walk me through the severance package, please?" "Who should I contact if I have questions about my 401(k) rollover?" "Can I count on you for a favorable reference?" "Would you be willing to fund any career coaching to help me through the transition?" "When will I receive my final paycheck?"

WHAT NEXT?

Try to keep a positive mindset as you move into the next phase of your career. If you have the luxury of taking some time off before diving into a job search, excellent. You might be amazed to discover how helpful a bit of rest and a clear head can be when making career decisions. If you need to land your next job ASAP, define your ideal next job *before* you edit your resume or start wildly applying for roles. A targeted, strategic approach will likely reap the best—and quickest—results.

You Are Dealing with Imposter Syndrome

Imposter syndrome—the inability to believe that your talents are real, or achievements deserved—is something many high-achieving people suffer from these days. If you have it, you feel anxiety, guilt, or depression, or are in constant fear of being exposed as a fraud or a phony. Whether you feel like this once in a while or every day, it's not an ideal way to operate, to say the least. Is there a solution?

 Try these ideas to address this issue:

1   **Open up to someone you trust.**
    If possible, find a fellow super-performer to confide in. They may know exactly how you're feeling and have some sound advice to offer.

2   **Flip the negative script in your head.**
    Do you honestly think your employer would have hired you if they felt you weren't the absolute best candidate for the job? Of course not. You've earned your spot. Remind yourself of this, daily.

3   **Celebrate your accomplishments.**
    Is your condition coming, in part, from your inability to give yourself credit for your wins? Own that magnificence—and take time to bask in your achievements, both big and small.

4   **Establish a practice of repeating affirmations (positive statements, such as "I've totally got this").**
    Positive affirmations can be an amazing tool for building up your self-confidence.

DON'T EXPECT A QUICK FIX. If you experience regular or chronic feelings of imposter syndrome, don't expect that a quick pep talk with a pal or telling yourself it's all in your head will deliver an instant cure. Changing faulty scripts of inadequacy requires conviction, hard work, and, potentially, support of a trained therapist. That said, it's well worth the effort. Having the weight of imposter syndrome lifted will improve your well-being and free you to deliver your best work.

HERE'S HOW Now that you have some tools and tips for evaluating and addressing imposter syndrome, here's something more to think about (and a few things to say).

Think This:

"There's an upside to falling short." Yes, really. Failure not only improves resilience; it can also serve as a tool in helping you overcome fear (which is what imposter syndrome is all about). When you realize that the fear of being "not enough" may actually *prevent* you from improving, you might feel compelled to take more risks...and, ultimately, enjoy more rewards.

Say This:

"My hard (and impressive) work has gotten me where I am today."

"It's no coincidence that I'm in this role. My boss believes in my capabilities... and my potential."

"Don't sell yourself short. You've got this."

"No one is expecting perfection. Take some risks, keep learning and growing, and have a little fun, for goodness' sake!"

WHAT NEXT?

If you can get past this idea that everyone is suddenly going to think you're unqualified and incompetent, you'll be able to focus on more important things, like making a genuine difference with your work. If you find it hard to eliminate the loop of negative self-talk, make yourself a "feel good file," fill it with the kudos and kind words you receive, and pull it out every time you need to remind yourself that you're pretty great after all. And if you still need help, ask a therapist for guidance.

You Are Experiencing Burnout

Burnout is an all-encompassing (physical, emotional, and mental) form of exhaustion that professionals, students, and really any human can experience. Some of the more typical signs of career burnout include loss of motivation or enthusiasm for your work, detachment, frequent irritability, and reduced productivity or performance. If that sounds familiar, what can you do to address it?

 Try these ideas to address this issue:

1 **Put out the fire.**
Burnout is no joke and, left unchecked, can lead to more serious mental health issues, increase your risk for illness, and jeopardize relationships. When you suspect burnout, make swift moves to find relief. Start by getting more sleep, eating healthier food, taking a mental health day, and so on. Listen to your body and act quickly.

2 **Learn to say no.**
It can be difficult to turn away someone in need, miss out on an opportunity, or risk looking unhelpful. But if you're fried, you've got to find ways to bow out of anything nonessential.

3 **Look for longer-range solutions.**
It doesn't stop at proper hydration and saying no. If your condition is severe—or you want to ensure burnout doesn't happen again—you'll need a variety of support and recovery resources. Delegate, join a gym, meditate, find a therapist. Do everything you can to restore your well-being.

DON'T TURN TO UNHEALTHY COPING MECHANISMS. As tempting as it may be to anesthetize yourself with things like alcohol, drugs, gambling, or other such means, these methods will likely just exacerbate your stress. Further, while it's natural to want to check out when things feel downright awful, the only way to get beyond burnout is to go through it. Healing is always better than ignoring. Apply this same principle to your burnout.

HERE'S HOW

As you digest these dos and don'ts, use these tips to support you through the recovery process.

Think This:

"I might need to adjust my default mindset to address this issue." Honoring your own needs comes very hard for a lot of people, especially those who are natural helpers or caregivers. But you can't be much of a helper or caregiver to anyone—colleagues, clients, family, friends—if you're doing so at the expense of your own basic needs. (There's a reason the flight attendant tells you to put your own oxygen mask on first.)

Say This:

"It's hard for me to admit this, but I'm burned out. I need some time off and hope you will support this."

"I didn't speak up until we got the deal closed, because I knew how important it was. It's crucial that I take a breather now."

"I need to delegate some of my accountabilities. Is this something you can help me with?"

WHAT NEXT? ⟶

If you're a high performer, you stand a reasonable chance that your employer will empathize with your situation, work with you to ease your immediate symptoms, and help you improve your work-life balance going forward. That's the ideal outcome. However, if you determine the job simply isn't conducive to your recovery, it's crucial that you weigh the costs/benefits of staying on your current path. An impressive job with plenty of challenge can be great, but if it comes at the expense of your well-being, is it really worth it?

You Have a Client Who Is Making Your Life Miserable

Spend enough time in the workforce, and you're bound to run into that one client with a talent for making your job—and life—a bona fide nightmare. They may be demanding, demeaning, or have unrealistic expectations. Perhaps they ignore deadlines, project scope, or that pesky invoice you sent four months ago. Difficult clients can drain your energy, waste your time, and end up costing your company, your team—and maybe even you personally—money. How can you deal with them?

 Try these ideas to address this issue:

1 **Get to the root of it.**
Is there anything underlying their behavior? And, as you assess the situation, ask yourself if you may be contributing to the contentious relationship. If so, own up, then take immediate steps to correct these things.

2 **Let them vent.**
If you determine your client is that explosive, reactionary type and/or one who seems to find a problem in *everything*, you may just want to let them get it out. Once they take a breath, calmly address their concerns. (Just don't allow any blatant abuse.)

3 **Establish firm boundaries.**
If your customer can't seem to see how they're overstepping, you'll be wise to spell out (in writing) project scope, what your available hours are, how you expect to be treated, etc.

4 **Fire them.**
If budget allows and you've exhausted all options in trying to improve the relationship—and your client is still sucking the life out of everyone—there's no shame in cutting ties.

DON'T LOSE YOUR TEMPER. It may seem impossible, especially if your client is a true hothead, a master manipulator, or someone you really can't stand. But, even if you get temporary satisfaction from unleashing on them, it probably won't help and you may also tarnish your reputation at work—or even lose your job. If you're finding it inconceivable to remain civil with a customer, remove yourself from the conversation as quickly and professionally as you can and revisit it later.

HERE'S HOW Beyond the basics, here are some additional ideas— and a few scripts to use—as you navigate an impossible customer scenario.

Think This:	Say This:
"I should try to be empathetic and patient—with my client *and* myself." Even if you let your client down, ticked them off, or created extra work for them, you can own up and try to mend fences. If it's not your fault, still try to find compassion. You never know what those people or that business is going through behind the scenes.	"Thank you for making me aware of how you feel. I understand why you're upset." "Here is our original agreement. It sounds like you may want us to expand the project's scope? If so, we can create a new proposal right away." "While my weekends are reserved for family time, I check my email first thing every Monday morning." "Your tone and words are threatening. Please don't speak to me like that."

WHAT NEXT?

If you manage to clear the air with your tough client, or find a more constructive way to interact, consider it a win. Remember what you said or did to achieve resolution. (It might come in handy down the road!) If they continue to drain your energy and focus—yet represent a crucial piece of business for your company—see if you can enlist a coworker to manage communications going forward. Maybe the change will help reset the relationship.

You Are Dealing with Harassment or Discrimination in the Workplace

While federal and (nearly all) state laws have prohibited harassment and discrimination in the workplace for decades, the issue (unfortunately) persists. And if you're being targeted by these behaviors at work, you know how serious of a problem they are. But the harm isn't limited to their direct victims—if you're witnessing these behaviors, you are still involved. Harassment and discrimination in the workplace are *everyone's* problem. We all have a part to play in addressing them—and working to eradicate them. How should you respond?

 Try these ideas to address this issue:

1 **If you've been the target:**
   If you feel safe in doing so, let the offender know how you feel. If not, remove yourself from the situation. Document and report the incident to HR. If HR ignores you, or the incident is minimized, go above that person until you feel heard.

2 **If you've witnessed it:**
   Speak up. Seek to understand, but don't let it slide. Let the perpetrator know their actions are unacceptable. Accept your responsibility in ensuring a safe and just workplace, even if you're afraid to make waves. (The law protects you from retaliation if you report, by the way.)

3 **If you're an employer:**
   Strive to create a culture of zero tolerance toward harassment and discrimination, and make your stance crystal clear to employees, new hires, customers, and vendors.

DON'T PRETEND HARASSMENT AND DISCRIMINATION AREN'T A BIG DEAL ANYMORE. They are. And, if you're not addressing them proactively—from the top down—you're going to erode employee trust, potentially lose business, and open yourself up for potential legal consequences. Harassment and discrimination can be overt or subtle, but for those at the receiving end, it's most assuredly not benign. You owe it to every single employee to identify and penalize all forms of it.

HERE'S HOW Here are some additional considerations and talking points around the topic of harassment and discrimination in the workplace.

Think This:

"As a professional, I have an obligation to conduct myself in a manner that's respectful of *all* people, at *all* times." If you were somehow raised or led to believe that people of certain cultures, genders, or races are "less than" in any way—or you have no issue with a playful pat on the rear end or a culturally offensive "joke"—then it's time to rethink things. Likewise, if you're inclined to turn a blind eye when you see an act of harassment or discrimination, consider how you may be perpetuating these extremely problematic acts by staying silent.

Say This:

"Do you realize that what you just said might come across as offensive?"

"What did you mean by that?"

"That was not funny."

"Don't touch me, please. It makes me feel uncomfortable."

"If this continues, I will go to HR or file an EEOC complaint."

WHAT NEXT?

Even if your efforts to put an end to harassment or discrimination result in a positive outcome (which, hopefully, they will), if you're the victim, you may struggle with residual aftereffects for weeks, months, or even years to come. Given this, it's imperative that you seek out any and all support resources you need to restore your well-being. Talk to a trusted friend, seek out professional help, and invest in self-care. And if your harasser doesn't stop, find a new position. Your well-being supersedes all else.

You Accidentally Share Confidential Information via Email

It can happen in a split second: You email top-secret data to the wrong Carlos or Charlene in your address book, or accidentally share an internal company financial document (instead of that adorable photo of your new puppy) with a client. We're all human, and these things can (and do) happen to the best of us. What's most important is knowing how to respond if it happens to you.

 **Try these ideas to address this issue:**

1 **Take some deep breaths.**
It'll be difficult, but try to remain calm and clear-headed.

2 **Try to recall the message.**
If you realize it immediately, you might be able to recall the message (if unopened). If you don't know how to do this, call the help desk or ask your boss right away.

3 **Contact the person you've accidentally sent it to and ask them to delete it immediately.**
Reasonable people understand that things like this happen, and they'll honor your request.

4 **Alert all necessary stakeholders as quickly as possible.**
Your manager, of course, should be the first to know. But, depending on what you've shared and the potential magnitude of the slipup, you may also need to get HR, legal, IT, or the PR teams involved.

DON'T PANIC AND DO NOTHING AT THE EXACT MOMENT YOU NEED TO BE DEMONSTRATING PEAK ACCOUNTABILITY. If you can't recall the message, the deed has been done. And the ripple effect could be notable (and include your being fired) if you opt to cut and run. When something like this happens, it's understandable that you'd rather pretend like nothing happened. But you've got to stand up and be accountable.

HERE'S HOW
Here are a few additional tips to help you as you scramble to respond to an immediate issue, or prevent future ones.

Think This:

"Can I change any process to avoid this in the future?" If it was that easy for you to send sensitive or private information to the wrong recipient(s), it might be time to rethink your digital filing system, email process (or offer to take the lead on implementing a companywide process), or other procedures. Brainstorm ideas, such as password-protecting certain files, to minimize your risks of this happening again.

Say This:

To your boss: "I'm so sorry, but I've just mistakenly sent confidential information to our client."

To the help desk representative: "I need to recall an email right now. Can you help?"

To the recipient: "I've sent you a sensitive file that I didn't intend to. Will you please delete the email immediately?"

To the legal team: "What are the most important next steps?"

WHAT NEXT?

Assuming you make it through this crisis in one piece, thank everyone who helped you resolve the issue and, again, explore how you can prevent a similar episode going forward. If the bottom does drop out as a result of your flub—and you get fired—practice how you'll answer the inevitable "Why'd you leave your last job?" question well in advance of your next interview. How do you do that? Be honest, focus on the lessons learned, then shift the conversation to the great things you have to offer!

You Need to Figure Out If It's Time to Find a New Job

Sometimes the itch comes a few months into a position; sometimes it's a few years. You start feeling a little bored or unmotivated, or you find yourself wishing you were doing something else. Is it time for a new job? Will something else be better than what you have now? There are more questions than answers in that situation. But if you're feeling that you've outgrown your job or that it no longer aligns with your goals or needs, what should you do?

 Try these ideas to address this issue:

1 **Take the "Sunday test."**
Do you start feeling very edgy, irritable, or anxious every Sunday? If the approaching workweek makes you feel awful, don't ignore this.

2 **Ask yourself if you've got room to grow in your current job or at your current employer.**
If no, are you okay with this?

3 **List the things you learned at work recently.**
If you're having a hard time with this assignment, that may mean it's time to move on.

4 **Evaluate the health of the company and industry.**
Are you in a growing firm or field? If so, great. If not, what might this mean in terms of job security or career trajectory?

5 **Define where you'd like to be in five years.**
Will staying in your current role help or hurt you in achieving that goal?

DON'T JUMP SHIP BECAUSE OF A FIXABLE PROBLEM. This book offers solutions for lots of common problems—which, once resolved, could render your current job fulfilling again. Job hunting, interviewing, getting references, negotiating terms...the whole process of finding a new job is a lot of work. If that's the best path, then go for it—but make sure you're ready for that commitment before you resign.

✔ HERE'S HOW

Now that you've got the basics, here's one more thing to think about and a few questions to ask if you're considering a new job.

Think This:	**Say This:**
"I may need to update my thinking on some old-school career beliefs." For example, if the thing holding you back from finding a new job is the fear that you've not been in your current role for long enough, here's a news flash: Fewer and fewer employers and recruiters are still hung up on the antiquated idea that "job hopping" is a bad thing. People change jobs, sometimes often, if it helps them advance and grow. In some industries, it's actually the norm!	"If I'm bored, are there ways to make my current job more challenging or interesting?" "If I'm worried, what do I need to find in a new job that will make me less concerned?" "If I'm anxious, how might a new job alleviate these feelings?" "If I'm falling off track of my five-year plan, what jobs will help me get back on course?"

WHAT NEXT? ───────────────────────────►

If you decide that it's time for a new job, great! Get excited about it. Feel confident in your ability to make thoughtful choices about your career and life. If, upon investigation, it seems that now is not the time, that's okay too. You're not giving up. You've done your assessment and made the choice that seems right for now. The road is long, and you can always revisit the issue in six months or a year to see if any circumstances have changed.

You Want to Move to a New City and Take Your Job with You

When you've got a hankering to move to another city, you might assume that you'll need to quit your current job and find something in your new location. And maybe you will. But wouldn't it be great if you could take the job that you love along for the ride? Thanks to the recent explosion in remote work opportunities, it may be entirely feasible. How can you broach the subject with your employer?

 Try these ideas to address this issue:

1. **Strategize on location.**
   If you suspect your employer may veto a fully remote option (and your company has multiple locations), consider targeting a city in which your company has another office.

2. **Create a proposal that makes actual business sense.**
   "I love palm trees and want to be in the warm weather" isn't going to sell anyone on this plan. You need a solid pitch—one that spells out all the benefits the company will reap if they approve your request.

3. **Consider how this might impact your career trajectory.**
   This is especially important if you're moving from company headquarters to a much smaller market or going fully remote.

4. **Be ready for a possible salary adjustment.**
   It may not come, but if you're moving to a less expensive town, your company could implement a cost-of-living salary reduction.

DON'T ASSUME THAT "YES" MEANS "YES FOREVER." It's going to be a bummer if you invest all kinds of time, money, and energy to move to another city only to discover that your employer's "work from anywhere" plan was indefinite or subject to things outside of your control—and now they definitely want everyone back in the main office. Be sure to get approval (in writing) from your manager.

HERE'S HOW Use the following additional tips and scripts as you build a plan and present your case.

Think This:

"I will be mindful of potential complexities." Even if it seems simple to you, it's not always seamless from the company's standpoint. For example, employers need to ensure that you're enrolled in the right healthcare plan (which likely differs state by state), that your tax information is accurate, and that your compensation aligns with the labor market where you reside. Go in knowing you might need to be patient and understanding of these logistical issues.

Say This:

"I've created a short presentation outlining how this could work. May I share it with you?"

"My research suggests that it will actually cost the company less if I'm working from this location."

"I've been working independently for a year now, so I'm hopeful you'll feel confident that this will be a seamless transition."

"I'm willing to fund (or co-fund) the move."

WHAT NEXT?

If your boss says yes, thank them and ask for their formal approval *in writing*. Then, as you settle into your new town, be sure to hold up your end of the bargain. If your request is denied, don't even consider moving anyway and praying that no one finds out. It's dishonest and could get you fired. Table the plan for now or start looking for a new job in your future hometown.

You Are Feeling Like You May Be in the Wrong Career Field

It's an incredibly fish-out-of-water moment. You realize that you've invested countless hours, endless energy, and maybe even tens of thousands of dollars to get to where you are professionally—and you're now fairly certain your chosen field no longer suits you. Maybe it's the actual job tasks, the pay scale, or the company's vision—something important just isn't syncing with you anymore. You have no idea what to do with this information, but ignoring it doesn't seem to be an option. What now?

 Try these ideas to address this issue:

1. **Ask yourself if it's a passing thought, or a feeling that will likely persist.**
Pivoting your career can be quite an undertaking. You'll surely want to honor your aspirations, but make sure you're not confusing "mad at my boss" with "definitely in wrong spot."

2. **Do some soul searching.**
Knowing you're in the wrong spot is a start. Now what? Spend as much time as you need to define what it is you want next, and what you don't.

3. **Meet with people working in careers you find appealing.**
No need to guess what a new field may be like; invite people working in those jobs to coffee or an informational interview.

4. **Try before you buy.**
If feasible, seek out volunteer work in a field of interest or offer pro bono services to a small business.

DON'T DO ANYTHING IMMEDIATELY (UNLESS YOU'RE IN A NOTABLY UNHEALTHY JOB SITUATION). Even if you're feeling antsy or disenchanted at work, avoid making an impulsive jump into an entirely new career field before doing some investigating. It's easy to get all starry-eyed about this profession or that, but until you give it your due diligence, you probably know little about what the day-to-day will feel like, or what it takes to succeed in that new arena. This is your career, and it probably means a lot to you. Give it the time and focus it deserves.

✓ HERE'S HOW

Once you've set up your first moves, use these tips and thought starters to ensure your exploratory conversations are a success.

Think This:

"I'm not stuck here forever." Feeling like you've been following the wrong career path can be upsetting, especially before you know what to do next. But you're simply not trapped (unless you tell yourself you are). If you look around, you will find plenty of people who ditched their "expected" or "planned" careers to do very different things. Talk to them. You may find their insights quite valuable in helping you shift your mindset and prepare for your future.

Say This:

"Do I want my boss's job, or the role that would likely come next for me?"

"If I leave, what 'missing aspects' will I be looking for in this next career move?"

"Can I afford to potentially step back income-wise while learning a new field?"

"Can I find career fulfillment without making a drastic move?"

WHAT NEXT? →

If, after giving things thorough consideration, a career pivot seems like the best next move, carefully craft your strategy and a game plan to help you get from where you are now to where you want to be. If you're still feeling stuck, consider enlisting the help of a professional career coach who has helped others through career changes. They can help you assess your current situation and strategize the best way forward.

RESOURCE LIST

Finding and Starting a New Job

Find Your Dream Job

Hosted by Mac Prichard of Portland, Ore.-based Mac's List, *Find Your Dream Job* is one of the best podcasts for anyone looking for their first job, searching for career direction, or in need of tools and resources to support their job search.

Jobscan

Jobscan (www.jobscan.co) is a nifty tool that enables job seekers to measure the algorithmic strength of their resumes—and optimize them—before submitting their resumes for consideration via online job application.

LinkedIn Learning

LinkedIn Learning (www.linkedin.com/learning/) is a massive open online course provider offering thousands of expert-led video courses on myriad business, creative, and technology topics. (Find Jenny Foss's job search–related LinkedIn Learning courses here: www.linkedin.com/learning/instructors/jenny-foss.)

The Muse

The Muse (www.themuse.com) is a robust resource for career advice, coaching services, and researching potential employers.

Self Made Millennial

Hosted by HR recruiter Madeline Mann, Self Made Millennial (www.youtube.com/c/SelfMadeMillennial/about) is a popular—and quite useful—*YouTube* channel featuring regular videos on everything from salary negotiation and informational interviews to recovering from major career or job search mistakes.

Dealing With Your Boss

Ask a Manager

Run by work advice columnist Alison Green, *Ask a Manager* (www.askamanager.org) tackles reader questions on formidable workplace and management issues.

Career Contessa

This lively blog and *YouTube* channel (www.youtube.com/watch?v=xpJVL6pLnlM) covers a wide range of career development topics, including plenty of great tips on dealing with bosses, both the good ones and the not-so-good ones.

Science of People

Run by behavioral investigator and body language expert Vanessa Van Edwards, *Science of People* (www.scienceofpeople.com) provides scores of science-backed people-skills tips and lessons to help professionals survive and thrive in the workplace.

Managing Your Coworkers

Beating the Workplace Bully: A Tactical Guide to Taking Charge

In *Beating the Workplace Bully*, author Lynne Curry, a longtime management consultant and HR trainer, shares tips on how to avoid, confront, and stay calm in the face of an office bully.

Dear HBR

Cohosted by Alison Beard and Dan McGinn, *Dear HBR* is an advice show for workplace dilemmas (including this episode on disagreeable colleagues: https://hbr.org/podcast/2020/02/disagreeable-colleagues).

Advancing Your Career and Becoming the Boss

Good Boss, Bad Boss: How to Be the Best...and Learn from the Worst

By *New York Times* bestselling author Robert I. Sutton, *Good Boss, Bad Boss* provides an eye-opening look at the traits of great bosses, and shares research-backed tips on how to deal with bad bosses.

How Highly Effective People Speak: How High Performers Use Psychology to Influence with Ease

Written by well-known public speaking coach Peter Andrei, *How Highly Effective People Speak* is a helpful primer for anyone looking to be at the top of their game when asking for a raise, disagreeing with your manager, or advocating for yourself through difficulty.

Work It Daily

Founded by longtime HR leader, recruiter, and career coach J.T. O'Donnell, Work It Daily (www .workitdaily.com) is a virtual career growth club that provides its members access to career coaching services, courses, and a membership community.

Handling Other Workplace Dilemmas

As We Work

Formerly hosted by Tess Vigeland, a longtime journalist and the author of *Leap: Leaving a Job with No Plan B to Find the Career and Life You Really Want*, *As We Work* is a weekly podcast that examines the changing dynamics of the workplace. (Check out this episode about burnout: https://open.spotify .com/episode/4riU0PLdQv4dU5U w3RLDSz.)

Dr. Dawn on Careers

Hosted by Dr. Dawn Graham, career change coach and Career Director for the Executive MBA program at The Wharton School at the University of Pennsylvania, *Dr. Dawn on Careers* is a SiriusXM Radio (channel 132) show that answers the job search, career pivot, and career development questions of listeners calling in.

"7 Important Books for Building an Anti-Racist Workplace"

Fast Company's recommended reading for building a truly inclusive workplace: www.fastcompany .com/90512400/7-important-books- for-building-an-anti-racist-workplace.

So Good They Can't Ignore You: Why Skills Trump Passion in the Quest for Work You Love

Written by Cal Newport, associate professor of computer science at Georgetown University, *So Good They Can't Ignore You* will change the way you think about how to find long-term career fulfillment. An essential for anyone pondering a career change.

INDEX

ABOUT THE AUTHOR

Jenny Foss is a longtime recruiter, job search strategist, and the founder and CEO of the internationally recognized career website JobJenny.com. She has been featured in leading publications, including *Forbes*, *USA TODAY*, *Fast Company*, and *Inc.*, and partners with LinkedIn in developing career-focused video courses for their LinkedIn Learning platform, with titles including "Resume Makeover," "A Career Strategist's Guide to Getting a Job," and "Expert Tips for Answering Common Interview Questions."

Through all of her work, Jenny aims to provide exceptional, accessible, and easy-to-act-upon advice that enables people to thrive in their careers. A Detroit native, unlikely hot yoga enthusiast, and Certified Professional Resume Writer (CPRW), Jenny lives in Portland, Oregon, with her husband, three kids, and rescue dog, Daisy.

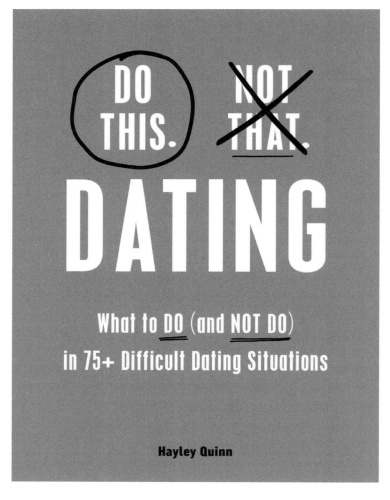